Simon Blackburn is the Professor of Philosophy at Cambridge University. He is the author of many philosophical works, including *Spreading the Word: Groundings in the Philosophy of Language* (1984), *Ruling Passions: A Theory of Practical Reasoning* (1998), and the *Oxford Dictionary of Philosophy* (1994, 2nd ed. 2005). His books bringing philosophy into public notice include *Think: A Compelling Introduction to Philosophy* (1999), *Being Good: A Short Introduction to Ethics* (2001), *Lust: The Seven Deadly Sins* (2004), *Truth: A Guide for the Perplexed* (2005), and *Plato's Republic: A Biography* (2006).

HOW TO READ

HUME

SIMON BLACKBURN

GRANTA

Granta Publications, 12 Addison Avenue, London W11 4QR

First published in Great Britain by Granta Books, 2008

Copyright © Simon Blackburn, 2008

A CIP catalogue record for this book
is available from the British Library.

1 3 5 7 9 10 8 6 4 2

ISBN 978 1 84708 033 2

Printed and bound in Great Britain
by CPI Bookmarque, Croydon

CONTENTS

SERIES EDITOR'S FOREWORD

How am I to read *How to Read*?

This series is based on a very simple, but novel idea. Most beginners' guides to great thinkers and writers offer either potted biographies or condensed summaries of their major works, or perhaps even both. *How to Read*, by contrast, brings the reader face to face with the writing itself in the company of an expert guide. Its starting point is that in order to get close to what a writer is all about, you have to get close to the words they actually use and be shown how to read those words.

Every book in the series is in a way a masterclass in reading. Each author has selected ten or so short extracts from a writer's work and looks at them in detail as a way of revealing their central ideas and thereby opening doors on to a whole world of thought. Sometimes these extracts are arranged chronologically to give a sense of a thinker's development over time, sometimes not. The books are not merely compilations of a thinker's most famous passages, their 'greatest hits', but rather they offer a series of clues or keys that will enable readers to go on and make discoveries of their own. In addition to the texts and readings, each book provides a short biographical chronology and suggestions for further reading, Internet resources, and so on. The books in the *How to*

Read series don't claim to tell you all you need to know about Freud, Nietzsche and Darwin, or indeed Shakespeare and the Marquis de Sade, but they do offer the best starting point for further exploration.

Unlike the available second-hand versions of the minds that have shaped our intellectual, cultural, religious, political and scientific landscape, *How to Read* offers a refreshing set of first-hand encounters with those minds. Our hope is that these books will, by turn, instruct, intrigue, embolden, encourage and delight.

Simon Critchley
New School for Social Research, New York

REFERENCES TO HUME'S WORKS

For ease of reading, in quoting Hume I have slightly modernized his eighteenth-century orthography: His 'deriv'd', 'produc'd', etc. become 'derived', 'produced'; ''tis' becomes 'it is' and ''twill' becomes 'it will'; and 'wou'd' and 'cou'd' become 'would' and 'could'.

The following abbreviations of titles of Hume's works are used throughout. (For details of the editions used, please refer to the Bibliography.)

D   *Dialogues Concerning Natural Religion.* References are to the dialogue number, from 1 to 12, followed by paragraph number, e.g. *D* 12.7.

E   *An Enquiry Concerning Human Understanding.* References are to section and page number, e.g. *E* 7, p. 144.

EM   *An Enquiry Concerning the Principles of Morals.* References are to part and paragraph number, followed by page number, e.g. *EM* 6.21, p. 125.

EMP   *Essays: Moral, Political, and Literary.* References are to the title of the essay followed by page number, e.g. 'The Sceptic', *EMP*, p. 166.

ST   'Of the Standard of Taste'. References are to paragraph number and page number in *EMP*, e.g. *ST* 7, p. 229.

T   *A Treatise of Human Nature.* References are to book, part, and section number, in that order, followed by page number, e.g. T I.iv.2, p. 216.

INTRODUCTION

Hume is the greatest British philosopher. But he is also the most perplexing. In this short book I hope to help the reader to understand how both these things can be true, for it is only when we work through the things that make Hume perplexing that we discover the things that make him great. He is also certainly the most loved of British philosophers, and perhaps, along with Socrates, the most loved of philosophers anywhere. His writings radiate the same calm, clear-sighted benevolence for which he was celebrated in his own life. It was not for nothing that in 2000, he was voted Scotsman of the millennium by his fellow countrymen, an honour that would have especially gratified him, for his country as well as himself.

David Hume was born in 1711 in the Scottish borders, and died in 1776 in Edinburgh, where he had lived for much of his life. He spanned the middle years of the eighteenth century, and he was a central figure of what was later recognized as the Scottish Enlightenment, the great flowering of arts and sciences that was pivotal in creating the modern world. He was educated at Edinburgh University, and after unsuccessful attempts at a career in business and law, still aged only twenty-three, he left Britain to live cheaply in rural France. Here, over the course of two years, in the little town of La Flèche, near Angers in rural France, he composed his greatest philosophical work, *A Treatise of Human Nature*.

He returned to Britain to see this through the press (1739), and settled into a literary life in Edinburgh. The first volume of his *Essays: Moral, Political, and Literary* was published in 1742, followed by *An Enquiry Concerning Human Understanding* (1748, often referred to as 'the first *Enquiry*') and *An Enquiry Concerning the Principles of Morals* (1751). His groundbreaking *History of England* was published in six volumes between 1754 and 1762. His *Four Dissertations* of 1757 included *The Natural History of Religion*, and his final, posthumous philosophical text is the delightful *Dialogues Concerning Natural Religion*, which Hume refused to make public in his lifetime, probably in order to avoid the outrage of the faithful, but instructed his heirs to publish after his death. His philosophical and literary life was punctuated by occasional forays into the wider world, notably as Secretary to the Embassy in Paris from 1763 to 1766, where he was lionized as a leading figure of the European Enlightenment: the leading philosophical interpreter of modern science, the empiricist who had brought the methods of that science into the study of human beings, the sceptic who had crushed the favourite arguments of religious thinkers, and the moralist and political theorist whose calm, benign understanding of human nature paved the way towards a new future.

Hume has always been misunderstood. Immanuel Kant, the first great philosopher to take his measure, writing only a few years after his death, named and shamed four of his more prominent opponents:

> But fate, ever ill-disposed toward metaphysics, would have it that Hume was understood by no one. One cannot without feeling a certain pain, behold how utterly and completely his opponents, Reid, Oswald, Beattie and finally Priestley missed the point of his problem and constantly misjudged his hints for improvement – constantly taking for granted just what he doubted, and conversely, proving with vehemence and, more often than not, with great insolence exactly what it had never entered his mind to doubt.[1]

Yet Hume took great pains with his style, especially after what he regarded as the failure of the *Treatise*, and he consciously wrote in order to reach as many readers as possible. He invented no new philosophical vocabulary and no fanciful categories. His abstract ideas and arguments are tempered with homely examples. He does not bludgeon the reader: on the contrary, like Plato, he is typically tentative and questioning, in dialogue with the reader and with himself. His later writings, especially the *Enquiry Concerning the Principles of Morals*, have an air of relaxed sunshine about them, a classic poise and pace that was easier to attain in the confident eighteenth century than in the more conflicted and insecure times that followed it. But that, one might have thought, would make his message all the more transparent. His prose, it is true, is rounded and expansive, in an eighteenth-century manner, but this by itself should not be much of an obstacle.[2]

It is when we try to absorb his ideas and to understand his message, in other words when we try to read him properly, that problems arise. In this short book we encounter those problems in the context of ten of the most important moments in Hume's philosophy. Inevitably, that leaves other contributions of his untouched, including seminal contributions on the metaphysics of space and time, the problem of freedom and responsibility, and much else. For his essays and writings encompass much more than philosophy: he made equally fundamental contributions to history, economics, political science, and demography. But the foundation of it all was the science of human nature, and it is with this that we start.

1

THE SCIENCE OF MAN

There is no question of importance, whose decision is not com-
prized in the science of man; and there is none, which can be
decided with any certainty, before we become acquainted with
that science. In pretending, therefore, to explain the principles of
human nature, we in effect propose a compleat system of the sciences, built on a foundation almost entirely new, and the only one
upon which they can stand with any security.

And as the science of man is the only solid foundation for the
other sciences, so the only solid foundation we can give to this
science itself must be laid on experience and observation.

T Introduction, p. xvi

Hume's philosophy was anthropocentric, through and through. His
subject was not 'the nature of the world', but what we human
beings make of the nature of the world. In other words, his subject
was human nature and human understanding. He believed that
while the science of nature had made spectacular advances, notably
through the kind of triumph gained in physics and mechanics by
Newton, the science of human nature had yet to catch up. He also
believed that since all sciences 'lie under the cognizance of men,
and are judged of by their powers and faculties', the understanding
of those powers and faculties could claim a fundamental status,
underpinning the achievements of other studies. He thought this
was obviously true of politics, morals, and 'criticism' or aesthetics,

fairly obviously true of religion, and even if it is less obvious, still true of mathematics and natural sciences. So his original ambition in philosophy was to lay the foundation of the science of man. It was to delineate the powers of the mind, the limits of understanding, the extent of our possible knowledge, and then to add a theory of our passions and motivations which would put morals and politics, just as much as natural science and mathematics, onto a firm foundation.

As we follow Hume's pursuit of this aim, there are two key words of his to hold onto: *nature* and *scepticism*, although each needs careful qualification. Indeed, in the latter case Hume gives the qualification himself, admitting only to a *mitigated scepticism*. Each of these gets much more attention later on: in this first chapter, I simply want to illustrate a general tone or shading they give to Hume's work. The emphasis on nature sets the entire course of his philosophy. It means that Hume sees human beings as animals like others: creatures with a variety of habits, including mental habits, and of course with 'passions' of which the simplest are things like fear and hunger. Our endowment consists of natural faculties that enable our lives to go forward in the environments in which we find ourselves. This ecological and, as we shall discover, Darwinian perspective gives Hume a relaxed attitude to ordinary mechanisms of living. We naturally pursue the objects of our passions, and in order to do so we trust our eyes, our senses in general, memory, elementary processes of generalization, unambitious predictions, and interpretations of our experience. We have no option about any of that. We did not design ourselves, and we cannot undo what nature has done. We can, it is true, modify it in some ways by learning and culture, but Hume is consistently suspicious of both the practicality and the wisdom of fighting against nature.

Hume's mitigated scepticism is the other side of this coin. It comes after Hume's utterly negative results when he tries by reasoning to underwrite the confidences that nature gives us. It turns out that reason, the darling of previous philosophers from Plato through to Locke or Spinoza, the distinguishing glory of human beings, and, in some philosophers of the century before Hume, even the quality in which we most closely resemble God, can neither generate our natural beliefs, nor underwrite them as adequate or valid.[3] On the contrary, reason's verdict on the beliefs that are most central to our lives, namely those in which we describe the spatially extended world about us, is that they cannot possibly be true. And on others about which it is not quite so damning, its verdict remains open: there is no reason for supposing them true. So except in trivial matters the light of reason proves to be a flickering guide, unstable and unreliable. Reason even undermines itself: when we reason carefully about reasoning, we arrive at the most sceptical, nihilistic view of it. So it is fortunate that nature bypasses it. Reason by itself would paralyse us, leaving us with no convictions or beliefs, and incapable of action. Nature steps in to take its place, forcing our minds and our motives into the shapes they have. For Hume, the human being is no longer the darling, even the fallen darling, of the cosmic order, the pinnacle of a rational plan executed by a benevolent deity who built us in his own image, but a struggling, not terribly well-equipped, and not terribly nice animal fighting for its niche alongside other human beings, with whom, when things go well, it is just about able to cooperate in a fragile social order.

Perhaps the radical nature of this vision of the human condition is best appreciated if we contrast it with that of Kant, who devoted his greatest work, *The Critique of Pure Reason* (1781), to trying to overcome it. Kant conceived his task as providing a 'deduction', in the lawyer's sense of the proof of title to a piece of property, for our basic categories of thought. It would not be enough to show that they are natural to us, or that we have no alternative and cannot but employ them. The question still remains of whether they are 'objectively valid', leading us to an insight into the actual way of the world, rather than screening us off from that with mere illusions. Thus Hume left us with conclusions such as these: we are minded to think that every event has a cause; we find it natural to believe in an objective order of events in space and time; we expect the future to resemble the past. Kant wanted to move from us being *minded* to think in such ways to us being *right* to think in those ways. He wanted to restore the harmony between our confidence and the truth. Kant's heroic wrestling with this task is a large topic, but here it suffices to say that he accomplishes it only at the cost of making the world itself a kind of 'construction'. Our thoughts are guaranteed to correspond to the world because the world as we apprehend it is in some dark sense fashioned by the way we think of it. This is 'transcendental idealism', and it has the consequence that the things we take ourselves to perceive and think about 'are in all their configurations and alterations nothing but mere appearances, that is, representations in us, of the reality of which we are immediately conscious'.[4] Hume did not live to respond to this, but he would unquestionably have said about it what he said about idealism in the work of Bishop Berkeley, that it is unbelievable. The price is too high. If this is what it takes to give reason its authority to guide our belief, once again, so much the worse for reason.

On the other hand, Hume shares much with Kant. In each of them, it is our own judgements, the products of our cognitive (and emotional) natures, that form the data for philosophical inquiry. And each of them recognizes that we cannot simply pat ourselves on our backs, awarding ourselves the right to dogmatic confidence that our judgements are in any sense nature's own. For Kant, this prompts the crisis of scepticism, and as we have seen, the need for a 'deduction' or proof of title. For Hume it prompts an attitude much nearer to modern pragmatism or 'neo-pragmatism', as it appears in the work of writers such as Richard Rorty,[5] who counsel that the very best that can be said about this or that aspect of our cognitive functioning, the last word and final verdict is – that it functions. If it works, and in any case we cannot think any other way, then that is all the deduction of title that we need or can provide.

Kant is absolutely correct that Hume's contemporary readers, including Thomas Reid and James Beattie, failed to understand that Hume's scepticism was directed towards the power of reason, not towards our natural beliefs. So they saw him as 'leaving no ground to believe any one thing rather than its contrary', which of course would make his positive ambition, of grounding a science of human nature, completely impossible. Here is Thomas Reid:

> It seems to be a peculiar strain of humour in this author, to set out in his introduction, by promising, with a grave face, no less than a complete system of the sciences, upon a foundation entirely new, to wit, that of human nature; when the intention of the whole work is to shew, that there is neither human nature nor science in the world. It may perhaps be unreasonable to complain of this conduct in an author, who neither believes in his own existence, nor that of his reader; and therefore could not mean to disappoint him, or to laugh at his credulity.[6]

But Hume does believe in his own existence and that of his reader, and many other things besides. He is not the 'monster of scepticism' that Reid thought. Hume is consistently scornful of what he calls 'Pyrrhonian scepticism', after the Greek sceptic Pyrrho of Elis. This doctrine shares the scepticism about reason, but goes on to conclude that the right course is to suspend judgement about everything. Hume simply replies that it cannot be done: nature is too strong for us, so such advice is futile. He is instead a mitigated sceptic, cautious and beset by an awareness of human fallibility, indeed, but entirely within his rights to offer a positive philosophy of his own. Whereas Reid and the others thought he was driving the empiricist principles he inherited from Locke and Berkeley to their ultimate absurdity, Pyrrhonian scepticism, he was in fact engaged on charting the mechanisms of the mind, of which they had no inkling, which restore everyday confidences to us in spite of the negative assessment of reason itself.

With this much understanding of Hume's general orientation, we can return to the perplexities that arise in reading him, and the air of instability or even inconsistency about the things he seems to be saying that make interpretation difficult and afford some excuse to Reid and his companions. To illustrate what I mean, here are some of the things that he seems to hold. He is an empiricist, who asserts that all our ideas must bear a very close connection to our experience – yet he cheerfully employs notions which, he also argues, bear no such connection to experience. He holds that the existence of a common-sense external world is something that must be taken for granted in all our reasonings – yet that elementary reflections show that it hides insoluble contradictions, and therefore cannot possibly be true. He holds a doctrine of 'natural belief', that while sober beliefs based on perception and memory are natural to us, they are no more rational than the wildest fancies – yet he also holds that wild fancies, such as beliefs in prophecies and miracles, are to be condemned and not to be held. He argues that for all we know in advance, anything may cause anything – yet he also holds that representations of the way of the world cannot by themselves motivate us to action. He holds that morality was nothing but an expression of our sentiments, which cannot be said to be either true or false – yet he also holds that nobody can honestly deny the reality of moral distinctions. He venerates Isaac Newton as the greatest ornament of the English nation – yet holds that science does nothing but stave off our ignorance for a little longer. He thinks that religion should properly be a subject of amusement more than anything else, and even says that when he hears that a man accedes to being a Christian, he, Hume, concludes he is a rascal – yet he also seems friendly to the argument to design for the existence of God, in spite of this being an argument which he has himself decisively demolished. He has an eighteenth-century, Enlightenment confidence in the uniformity of human nature – yet in his history and his essays he constantly returns to the existence of cultural difference and divergence.

Some of these alleged inconsistencies are superficial and easily resolved. Hume also wrote with rhetoric and irony, and sometimes he overstates his views. He distinguished between strict and philosophical inquiry, and the relaxed language of everyday thought, and it is essential to see which voice he is allowing himself at any particular point, and to set individual sayings in their context. His idiom is not that of modern professional philosophy, which strives for a strict, rigid order of expression, constantly fighting (often unsuccessfully) against the mobile, fluid, and rhetorical nature of language.

But other puzzles have deep sources in Hume's view of things. Apparent inconsistency in a great philosopher signifies a point of stress: a point where he, and we, cannot see how things hang together, and have to cope with some rupture in our view of the world and of our place in it. Perhaps the rupture only arose from some views that prevailed at the time of the writer, and the greatness lay in overcoming it. This is the way that in the following century the optimistic Hegel sees human self-consciousness advancing, as previous contradictions are overcome in the advances of history. But the deeper problems lie where we cannot simply abandon old ways of thinking, or joyfully commit ourselves to new, trouble-free conceptual schemes, or new, clean, scientific vocabularies. They lie where we cannot see what such new ways of thinking could possibly be like, nor how they could possibly help (think of the intractable problems of understanding consciousness or free will). Hume had an extraordinary ability to reveal these fractures, not only in the prevailing thought of his own time, but in the thought of our own time, and for all we can imagine, of any time. We cannot reason our way past them: this is the crux of Hume's assault on the powers of reason. As a result, a certain instability in our position is inevitable. It is the same kind of instability that later excited Friedrich Nietzsche, and it is useful to think of Hume in the light of the emphasis on the perpetual work of human perspective that Nietzsche also highlighted.[7] Thus Hume concludes the first book of the *Treatise* defending the practice of philosophical reflection, but in the following surprisingly modern or postmodern terms:

Nor is it only proper we should in general indulge our inclination in the most elaborate philosophical researches, notwithstanding our sceptical principles, but also that we should yield to that propensity, which inclines us to be positive and certain in *particular points*, according to the light, in which we survey them in any *particular instant*. It is easier to forbear all examination and enquiry, than to check ourselves in so natural a propensity, and guard against that assurance, which always arises from an exact and full survey of an object. On such an occasion we are apt not only to forget our scepticism, but even our modesty too; and make use of such terms as these, *it is evident, it is certain, it is undeniable*; which a due deference to the public ought, perhaps, to prevent. I may have fallen into this fault after the example of others; but I here enter a *caveat* against any objections, which may be offered on that head; and declare that such expressions were extorted from me by the present view of the object, and imply no dogmatical spirit, nor conceited idea of my own judgment, which are sentiments that I am sensible can become no body, and a sceptic still less than any other. (*T* I.iv.7, p. 273)

We may achieve equilibrium on particular points at particular instants of time, but we must constantly remind ourselves that if we follow a neighbouring train of thought we might come to quite a different result, indeed that this is inevitable given the fallibility of weak human reason. And this, Hume did think, would check and mitigate any tendencies to pride and dogmatism – a lesson that our own time would do especially well to hear.

In connection with morals there is the same combination of scepticism about reason with naturalism about our motivations and desires. Here, however, the result is not at all pessimistic. Hume has no rose-tinted spectacles when it comes to human nature. All he requires is that there is 'some particle of the dove, kneaded into our frame, along with the elements of the wolf and the serpent' (*EM* 9.4, p. 147). He describes a partially selfish, partially sympathetic human nature, able to take into account a point of view in common with others, and able to evolve institutions that increase its security, happiness, convenience, and pleasure. All that is excellent, and a cause for a certain self-congratulation. And anything that threatens those institutions is to be feared and resisted.

This brings into view another rock on which a reading of Hume might founder. The celebration of what comes naturally might to a careless eye seem to chime in with the later back-to-nature, 'noble savage' Romanticism of Jean-Jacques Rousseau, while the scepticism about the power of reason would similarly resonate with that philosopher's mistrust of reflection and design, vilified as the architects of the despicable, artificial world of civilization. But nothing could be further from Hume's attitude. Hume is thoroughly happy with the institutions that have evolved and the 'conveniences' of life which they make possible. He admires the mechanisms that have brought us where we are. Hume is intelligent enough to shudder at the realities glossed over by visions of the idyllic life of the noble savage, or the fiction of a golden age before the evolution of society, a world of human nature on all fours. There is no dreaming, and certainly nothing Romantic, about Hume. Politically, he is largely conservative, and especially suspicious of any presumption that by thought and design we can justify revolutions, and out of our own heads spin better systems than those that have evolved and stabilized over time. Hume was a radical in philosophy, not in politics.

The Enlightenment that Hume represents is often called the Age of Reason. And it was indeed an age in which thinkers in the West shrugged off the consolations of religion, and the divinity invested in monarchies and fixed authorities of all kinds, and looked instead to education and science for the task of constructing more just and democratic social orders. But even this overview shows us that by no stretch of the imagination can Hume be called an apostle of reason. He was a Darwinian before his time, an apostle, if anything, of evolved human nature and human sentiment. Instead, his commanding presence in philosophy lies in the clarity of his vision, the fact that time and time again he sees so exactly how things stand with us.

2

EMPIRICISM

Thus we find, that all simple ideas and impressions resemble each other; and as the complex are formed from them, we may affirm in general, that these two species of perception are exactly correspondent. Having discovered this relation, which requires no farther examination, I am curious to find some other of their qualities. Let us consider how they stand with regard to their existence, and which of the impressions and ideas are causes, and which effects.

The *full* examination of this question is the subject of the present treatise; and therefore we shall here content ourselves with establishing one general proposition, *That all our simple ideas in the first appearance are derived from simple impressions, which are correspondent to them, and which they exactly represent.*

T I.i.1, p. 4

Hume begins each of his major works of philosophy with a principle for linking 'ideas' in the mind with 'impressions', things that are also in the mind, but somehow different. He separates ideas into those that are 'simple' and those that are 'complex'. Simple ideas are 'such as admit of no distinction nor separation' (*T* I.i.1, p. 2). Complex ideas may be 'distinguished into parts'. So, to use his example, an apple unites together a particular colour, taste, and smell, and is in that sense a composite or complex, whereas the sensory qualities themselves are simple. We are able to 'put together' simple ideas in imagination, forming ideas of things like the apple, but also things that we may never have come across: 'I can imagine to myself such a city as the *New Jerusalem*, whose pavement is gold and walls are rubies, tho' I never saw any such' (*T* I.i.1, p. 3). But the simple ideas themselves are not the result of this compounding together. They are, as the italicized part of the quotation at the head of this chapter says, 'derived from simple impressions'. This principle is Hume's famous principle of empiricism, his 'derivation principle'. It is a descendant of the medieval thought that *nihil in intellectu quod non fuerit in sensu* – nothing is in the intellect or mind which was not in the senses. But Hume does not put it in terms of intellect versus sensory experience, but in terms of ideas and impressions.

At first sight, the derivation principle is very appealing. You can have the idea of redness, but only because you are acquainted with red things. You can have the idea of the taste of a peach, but only because you have tasted peaches. It is presumably only with the experience of the way our bodies move that we have an idea of what we can control and what we can't. It is surely attractive to suppose that it is only through our experience of time that we can think of time, and through our experience of space that we can think of space. If I tell you of zogs out there, but can do nothing to explain what connection zogs have to anything you can ever experience, you are going to be lost. This is so even in the sphere of physical theory. I may tell you that gravitational waves distort a metre length of an object by a small fraction of the diameter of the nucleus of an atom, and gain some hold on your imagination. You might *try* to measure it, to amplify it into a result you can perceive. But if I told you that the same wave did nothing that connects in any way with your actual or possible experience, then I have told you nothing.

Hume is certainly not to be faulted for putting some connection between thought and experience at the head of his work. His central aim is to give a theory of what we know and understand, and to remind us of what we do not know and may never understand.

The relationship between thought and experience is crucial on each front. If all our thoughts need some satisfactory pedigree in experience, or some certificate of authenticity that only experience can provide, then the project of delineating what we can understand has its launch pad. And if we can *only* know things that in turn have some satisfactory basis in experience, then that too should enable us to delineate the scope and limits of human knowledge. Hume is not the first or last philosopher to have looked for the right link in just such a relationship. John Locke before him, and a host of successors from Kant to Russell to the logical positivists of the early twentieth century and down to the present time, have acknowledged some need to find a way in which experience underwrites thought.

Impressions enter the mind with 'force or violence', and ideas are 'faint images of these in thinking and reasoning' (*T* I.i.1, p. 1). The difference is supposed to be one we can feel. Hume allows himself to consider only the experiences themselves, or something like their 'intrinsic' or felt nature, as opposed to the origins they may have. Presumably he takes this course because he does not want to hand himself too much of a common-sense understanding of the world at the outset of his inquiry. Such ideas as that of an external world full of independent objects at different spatial locations are going to be the subjects of theory, for the fact that we think in those terms is one which he wants his new science of human nature to investigate. And this prevents him from using anything other than the raw feel or phenomenology as data, at least in the beginning of the inquiry.

Some modern philosophers would say that starting with what is 'inner' to our minds derails the inquiry right at the outset. They would complain that it reflects a 'Cartesian' prejudice – so called because it was the method employed by the French philosopher René Descartes, especially in his influential *Meditations* of 1641 – according to which we know the contents of our own minds better than we know anything else, so that the job of philosophy is to erect an edifice of knowledge and understanding taking the internal as primary and everything else as secondary. And, they would continue, that is a thundering mistake. We cannot understand anything about our minds independently of understanding our situation in the public world. What we call 'thinking about our experience' is in fact thinking about such things as the way in which tulips or oranges look, or the way in which a violin sounds or a pineapple smells. Our experiences are only identifiable, and only possible objects of understanding, by way of our acquaintance with the world itself. In different ways, Ludwig Wittgenstein in Britain and Wilfrid Sellars in the United States spearheaded this general flight from the 'inner', and the reversal of the Cartesian priority.[8]

It would be depressing if this modern consensus relegated Hume's works to mere episodes in the history of ideas, primitive failures only there to be patronized by advanced philosophy. Fortunately it does not, because the way in which the derivation principle and the impressions/ideas distinction work in Hume is largely independent of anything that is objectionable in the Cartesian priority.[9] To see why, I shall shelve the Wittgensteinian or Sellarsian objection for a moment, and consider another general criticism of Hume's procedure.

The objection is that, if Hume expects his division between impressions and ideas to reflect the distinction between experience and thought, he is doomed to failure. He makes it seem as if the difference between, say, hearing a violin and imagining hearing a violin is like that between hearing the violin close by and hearing it far away, or hearing the violin and hearing an echo. The second experience is 'faint', and less 'lively' or 'strong' or 'vivid' than the first. Yet we find it easy to distinguish even the fainter experience from the mere imagining or remembrance of a violin. And in general, thinking about things is not like hearing them only with the volume turned down, or like seeing them only in a bleached-out, faded old photograph. The same philosophers who fell into line behind Wittgenstein and Sellars over the priority of the public were very quick to dismiss Hume for having a 'pictorial' theory of thinking, believing that thoughts are essentially faint pictures of how things are.

Why would this be such a mistake? Contemporary philosophers prefer to talk of concepts, rather than ideas, as elements of thought. And they are suspicious of equating the proper use of a concept with anything like a faint representation of a scene or a kind of echoing replay of an original experience. For by employing concepts we describe or interpret scenes, and to describe or interpret is not simply to rehearse: any rehearsal, vivid or faint, would require description or interpretation just as much as an original view or 'impression'. For example, if you heard a noise you didn't recognize, you would not gain an understanding of it simply through replaying it in your head. A mental replay might jog your memory, but that is all. So concepts are thought of more in terms of 'rules', and the ability they give us, of describing events, is seen as quite distinct from any passive sensory response to things. Description and interpretation are active processes.

The plot thickens if we suppose, as Kant taught, that these cognitive processes do not so much come after experience (although they can, as when you suddenly learn something new about what you are looking at) as that they more fundamentally *shape* experience. Kant alerted us to the kind of interpenetration of thought and experience that means that we typically see things as falling under various categories. For example, we see everyday things around us as solid, causally powerful, persisting, and cohesive individual items, with definite boundaries and places in space. Were we to try not to perceive them like this, we would probably fail, or, if we succeeded, the result would be very different from everyday perception. For Kant, the prime mistake of previous empiricists, like Locke and Hume, had been to 'sensualize' the understanding, assimilating the active role of conceptual interpretation to the passive reception of uncategorized experience. But it had also been to think of experience as itself uncategorized, a blank picture awaiting interpretation. For Kant, perception is itself partly an activity of thought. The way we perceive is infused with the way we think.

I certainly do not think Hume anticipated Kant's insights here. But it is not clear that anything he says shows him falling foul of

them either. Offering him a very simple pictorial model of the
relation of impressions and ideas is not reading Hume, but reading
things into him. We must certainly admit the Kantian distinction
between the reception of data through the senses and the ability to
interpret what is received, but Hume also struggled with the same
distinction and, as we shall see, approached it in terms highly con-
genial to recent philosophy of mind, that is, in terms of the
functions that thought brings with it. For the evidence is that he
had in mind something very different from anything merely pictorial, with ideas simply corresponding to a turning down of the
volume or a fading of the scene.

First of all, it is not clear at all that he thinks of 'ideas' as images,
or the kinds of thing that could be faded or bleached out, or faint
in the way that sounds and colours can be faint. In the *Enquiry* he
draws the contrast like this:

By the term *impression*, then, I mean all our more lively perceptions, when we hear, or see, or feel, or love, or hate, or desire, or
will. And impressions are distinguished from ideas, which are the
less lively perceptions, of which we are conscious, when we
reflect on any of those sensations or movements above mentioned. (*E* 2, p. 97)

This makes it clear that even things like feelings of love and
anger can be impressions. And there is no hint that in being
angry we are presented with an image of anything. What the
examples have in common is that they are all in some sense the
primary elements of our mental life, the ones that matter to us.
And that in turn suggests we reinterpret the vocabulary of
'vivacity' in *causal* terms. The obvious difference between feeling angry and merely thinking of someone being angry is that
the former makes me do things which the latter does not. And
similarly, seeing a snake in the path makes me alter course in a
way in which thinking of one as a possibility does not. The
impressions of the senses and the nature of our 'passions' directly
control the way we behave; thoughts and reflections about these

things do so at best indirectly.[10] This is in fact almost exactly what Hume says:

> An idea assented to *feels* different from a fictitious idea, that the fancy alone presents to us: And this different feeling I endeavour to explain by calling it a superior *force*, or *vivacity*, or *solidity*, or *firmness*, or *steadiness*. This variety of terms, which may seem so unphilosophical, is intended only to express that act of the mind, which renders realities more present to us than fictions, causes them to weigh more in the thought, and gives them a superior influence on the passions and imagination. (*T* Appendix, p. 629)

The idea, then, is that impressions function differently in our mental economy. They direct what we do in a way that reflections and ideas do not. In the end, Hume has in fact three categories to talk about. There are firstly impressions. Prominent among these are impressions of the senses, giving us perceptions of this or that object in our immediate environment, and representing these objects as having this or that property. Hume, like Locke, also thought we have impressions of 'reflection', that is, awareness of the contents of our own minds, but for the moment these can be put to one side. Secondly, there are ideas such as might arise when we reflect on the day's scenes. And thirdly, there are beliefs and memories. Hume sees the difference in each case in causal and functional terms. Beliefs and memories have more 'liveliness', meaning more causal power, more impact on us than mere imaginings. They direct more of our actions. They tell us what to expect, and direct our thoughts. But they do not direct action in the here and now in the way that perceptions do.

Given this functional understanding of these divisions, what can we make of the great principle of empiricism, the derivation principle, that all simple ideas must be derived from simple impressions? Why shouldn't the mind have in it some idea which is not itself compounded, a complex formed of other more simple ideas, but which just happened, occurred without being preceded by anything with the extra oomph that makes it an impression, on this causal criterion? Indeed, in one notorious passage Hume himself allows that this could happen. He gives the example of someone acquainted with a sequence of shades of a colour, without however having an impression of one particular shade, missing from the sequence. Hume allows that this person could conjure up an idea of the 'missing shade of blue'. But the case clearly does not interest him: he sees it as trivial, uninteresting in the context of the bigger game that he wants to hunt with the derivation principle.

The reason is that in this case, when the idea precedes the impression, it does so by enabling the subject to understand exactly *which* impression would manifest to him the object he is imagining – the missing shade. Here the imagining is running ahead of experience, but the subject knows how experience could catch up. But Hume is going to use the derivation principle precisely to make problematic those ideas where experience *couldn't* catch up. He is going to be interested in ideas which *couldn't* reveal their object in impressions. If we think of experience as providing a certificate of authenticity to our ideas, then these are ones which either cannot earn, or are going to have difficulty earning, their certificate. To anticipate some examples, he is going to convince us that we do not have a manifestation, in an impression, of a causal connection between distinct events. Hence, the very idea of such a connection is put into jeopardy. He is going to convince us that we do not have any impression of a self or subject of experience, and hence the idea of the self is put into doubt. He is similarly sceptical about any idea of substances as distinct from properties, and he is going to argue that the very idea of extended independent objects situated at a spatial distance from ourselves is not genuinely authenticated by experience.

To do this work the derivation principle ought not really to be stated in the way it is. It talks of impressions preceding ideas. But that is not the important link. The question of genesis or temporal priority is not where the action is. Whereas I said above that according to empiricism our thoughts needed some pedigree or certificate of authenticity in experience, we can now be more careful and distinguish the two. A *pedigree* would imply that the

thought must be the offspring of the experience. But a later
impression might satisfactorily *authenticate* an idea, as in the example of the missing shade. It would be a question of whether any
experience *could* acquaint us with the object of thought: the causal
connection, or the self, or the identity of objects through time, or
substances, or the fact that we ought to do something. We can
safely sideline any interest in temporal precedence. Indeed, we
shall see that to remain consistent to his own philosophy, Hume
himself ought to do so. He is in no position to insist, from the
armchair, that one kind of thing must precede or follow another,
since he holds that any two distinct and separate events could consistently occur in any order we like, or in no regular order at all. It
would be purely an empirical question, settled by seeing how
events actually fall out, whether any such thing happens or not.
But there may be more weighty reasons for doubting whether
some objects of thought could show themselves in experience at
all, and it is this big game that he goes on to chase.

Hume has his own views about the way in which ideas perform
something like the Kantian role, of bringing order into what
would otherwise be what William James called the 'blooming,
buzzing, confusion' of the infant's first experience, or what Kant
called the 'rhapsody of perceptions', which was what experience
might have been like without its shaping by our categories of
thought.[11] He holds that ideas become 'general in their representation', with the imagination presenting them 'at the very instant,
in which they become necessary or useful' (*T* I.i.7, p. 24). With
his functional account of thought in the background, we can gloss
this as emphasizing the facility with which we categorize and clas-
sify the passing show, and the utility of the interpretations that
automatically spring to mind. For an idea, in Hume, like a concept
in later writers, will prompt expectations and actions based on
them: seeing that it is a tiger, or seeing it *as* a tiger, prompts very
different reactions from seeing it as, or seeing that it is, a stuffed toy
or a piece of confectionery. He thinks that we have a capacity to
deploy the right kind of ideas. We need a classification appropriate to the kinds of generality we need, and Hume thinks that it is

a kind of 'magical faculty in the soul' that enables us to do that (*T* I.i.7, p. 24). His insight was later refurbished by Wittgenstein, who also invited us to wonder at the brute contingency underlying our shared, automatic capacity to extend the application of old words to just the right new cases.[12]

I have been emphasizing that we can, and should, read Hume as not at all out of touch with philosophies of mind and experience that are often thought to have supplanted him. And in that context it is worth remembering that Kant himself was preoccupied with the same question of legitimacy. For Kant, concepts needed authentication, through the legitimate work they do in enabling us to interpret experience: all knowledge requires the joint contribution of 'intuitions' or what is given by sense experience, and concepts. 'Concepts' that had no principled connection with the classification, explanation, or prediction of intuitions or sense experiences would be empty. Kant encapsulated his own empiricism in the famous slogan that 'without sensibility no object would be given to us, without understanding no object would be thought. Thoughts without content are empty, intuitions without concepts are blind.'[13] Hume is on the same track.

So we are left with Hume poised to ask how various elements of our thinking and understanding stand up to the empiricist test. Do our ideas or concepts earn their keep in helping with the categorization of experience? Or do they only provide some kind of fake show of understanding, tangling us in illusions of knowing what we are talking about, of having things understood and sorted out? And if our ways of thinking are not quite as spotless as we would like to think, what kind of remedy might we have, and how should the new science of human nature proceed? These questions plunge the reader into the most celebrated of all Hume's contributions to philosophy, his subtle and contested theory of the causal connection between events. It is here that empiricism begins to bite.

3

CAUSATION

There is, then, nothing new either discovered or produced in any objects by their constant conjunction, and by the uninterrupted resemblance of their relations of succession and contiguity. But it is from this resemblance, that the ideas of necessity, of power, and of efficacy, are derived. These ideas, therefore, represent not any thing, that does or can belong to the objects, which are constantly conjoined. This is an argument, which, in every view we can examine it, will be found perfectly unanswerable. Similar instances are still the first source of our idea of power or necessity; at the same time that they have no influence by their similarity either on each other, or on any external object. We must, therefore, turn ourselves to some other quarter to seek the origin of that idea ... The necessary connexion betwixt causes and effects is the foundation of our inference from one to the other. The foundation of our inference is the transition arising from the accustomed union. These are, therefore, the same.

T I.iii.14, pp. 164–5

Causation, power, necessity, and laws of nature are fundamental to our interpretations of the world, or any attempt to understand it. They are also the subject of Hume's most famous single contribution to philosophy. The quoted paragraphs are the climax of book I, part iii of the *Treatise*, Hume's longest discussion of these notions. Hume himself saw this discussion as the heart of his philosophy, and his principal claim to philosophical fame. In the *Abstract*, a short work he wrote advertising the *Treatise* to a public unhappily reluctant to purchase it, he describes this as the 'chief part' of the book, and more than half of the *Abstract* is devoted to it. It is the linchpin of Hume's attitude to natural science, to our capacities to predict and control nature, to our confidence in a world lying beyond the immediate reach of current experience, as well as to such problems as those of free will, the causal interaction between mind and matter, the reliability of human testimony, and attempts to argue for God as the cause of the universe.

So what is Hume's position? He first claims that we have no a priori knowledge of what events can cause what other events – no armchair knowledge of the particular causal powers of things, nor of any general principles of causation. These are not like the laws of arithmetic, or the principles of logic. The proof of this is simple: 'May I not clearly and distinctly conceive, that a body, falling from the clouds, and which, in all other respects, resembles snow, has yet the taste of salt or the feeling of fire?' (*E* 4, p. 115). There is no contradiction in imagining the most outlandish successions of events. A resourceful film director can illustrate the most extraordinary science fiction, in which ordinary events have utterly bizarre consequences, but even a George Lucas or Steven Spielberg cannot illustrate a circular square, or a person who simultaneously has three eyes and an even number of eyes. Contradictions cannot even be imagined to be true. But strange goings on are not like that. Anything consistent can be imagined to happen, we have to consult the ways of the world to find what does happen and what does not. The actual patterns of events are to be found not by rational thought but by empirical observation.

All we have to go on, then, in coming to causal interpretations of the world is the unfolding succession of events. But what do these events actually show us? According to Hume, as we apprehend them by means of the senses, they directly manifest or 'discover' empirical qualities. But they do not manifest or discover their causal powers and potentials. If they did, he argues, then we could know, just by contemplating an event by itself, what results to expect from situations where it occurs. But we cannot know this. We have to wait and see, finding by experience whatever the results may be.

Thus far, the argument will appeal to many philosophers and empirical scientists who have grown to prefer the cautious observations of the laboratory to a priori or armchair views about what must cause what, or what cannot cause what. But Hume then asks what empirical experience actually shows us. He argues that further experience only gives us a repetitive *pattern* of events. It too fails to disclose anything that really cements events together: real necessities, binding connections between distinct events. The causal powers of objects do not display themselves in any simple sensory way. We cannot just see smoking causing lung cancer, or genes causing hair growth, even if we are sure that these things happen.

In fact, many philosophers before Hume had denied that causation is manifest in the relations between events that we experience. As far back as the eleventh century the Arabic philosopher Al-Ghazali denied us empirical knowledge of causation, reserving all real causal power to the activity of God, who controls regularities in the world by treating some events as 'occasions' on which to bring about others himself – hence the title of the view, occasionalism. It was the favourite theory of one of the most distinguished French philosophers of the generation before Hume, and one whose work Hume knew intimately, Nicolas Malebranche. So it is not particularly radical of Hume to say that while the conjunction of events is open to view, their connection, whatever makes one a consequence of the other, remains hidden or 'secret'. The way events fall out just shows us, we might say, one damn thing after another. It is then *up to us* to interpret the sequence in terms of causation.

It is key to Hume's development of the argument that a repetition of some pattern of events cannot mean that it actually discloses anything new to us – anything not apparent in the single case. What we see once is what we see twice, and then again. But repetition matters. It effects a change in *us*, the observer. It can work on our psychologies. How does it do that? It generates a *functional* change, concisely summed up by saying that 'we make no longer any scruple of foretelling one upon the appearance of the other, and of employing that reasoning, which can alone assure us of any matter of fact or existence' (*E* 7, p. 144). The functional change is *not* that we become able to perceive the causal power of things, or gain an impression of why events 'must' fall into the patterns that they do. The change is just that we become skilled at foreseeing what events follow what others, and thereby of course at bringing things about or averting them, controlling events to our own advantage. Some of Hume's language suggests that it is an internal impression, an impression of 'reflection', that gives us the idea of causal necessity. But Hume does not mean this: he is adamant that the operations of our own minds reveal simply the brute conjunction or succession of events in our minds, just as observation of the external world reveals such conjunctions in the outside world. Hume is particularly severe on the idea that our own *agency* discloses any more. Berkeley had thought that our idea of causation was just that of our own will, our own ability to make things happen, and had drawn the consistent, if surprising, conclusion that only minds or spirits could make things happen.[14] Hume utterly rejects that. The change in our minds is just a new association, which becomes voiced or expressed as we make a causal interpretation of whatever we are observing. Causation is a kind of projection of our confidence that one kind of thing will follow another.

Hume ends both his major discussions of the matter with what he somewhat apologetically offers as 'two definitions' of cause. These are in fact not strict definitions, but they highlight the two different sides to the theory. There is what the world displays: regularities in the succession of events. And there is what the mind makes of it: the change that unites the two events in our imagination, so that '*the idea of the one determines the mind to form the idea of the other, and the impression of the one to form a more lively idea of the other*' (*T* I.iii.14, p. 172, also *E* 7, p. 146).

The theory, then, has four elements. There is, first, the innocent

mind, able to apprehend the sensible qualities of things, and to register patterns of happenings. There are the patterns themselves,
supplied by nature, in which some events are regularly followed, in
predictable ways, by others. There is the functional change in the
mind, which now becomes able to foresee changes about to
happen, when presented with the first part of a repeating pattern,
or to say what changes would happen, were the first element to
occur. And finally, there is the linguistic and cognitive expression of
that change, in the talk of causation, power, necessity, or force. But
none of this gives us any impression of causation, power, or necessity, and hence, by the empiricist principle, it does not furnish us
with any idea of what these might be either. Our understanding,
we might say, remains at the level of empirical patterns, but our
repeated exposure to such patterns gives us dexterity at handling
them – and that includes talking about them in causal terms.

The key point to grasp is that the theory is *metaphysically conservative*. The change in the mind Hume talks of is not a dawning
awareness of something new, some fact or relation between things.
There is nothing new in our field of view at all, and since there is
no new impression, there is no new idea of anything either. All
that there is instead is a change in our reactions: an increased facility in dealing with the kinds of events and properties and relations
of things of which we are aware. It may help to understand this if
we compare it with the identical kind of theory that Hume will
offer in the case of virtues and obligations, the stuff of ethics. Here
again there is the innocent mind, able to perceive an empirical situation. Again, there is a change in the mind due to the impression
or idea of the situation: in this case the arousal of a 'sentiment' or
'passion' of love or aversion, admiration or dislike. And finally,
there is the social practice of voicing these sentiments, which is
performed by our moral language. That is all there is to it. Again,
the theory is metaphysically conservative: there is no 'realm' of
ethical fact to which we have access, and no accompanying mys-
teries about what is responsible for this realm, or why we should
care about it, or how we manage to access it. There is only the
empirical world, and there are ourselves, able to register it, but also

able to react to it, and needing to voice and discuss our reactions with each other. Our propensity to 'ethicize' and our propensity to 'causalize' have exactly the same outlines.[15]

I have presented only the broad outline of Hume's view. There is room for a great deal of detail within the overall framework. Hume wonders, for instance, whether actual exposure to repetitions of pairs of events is always necessary to prompt us to think of a causal link between them, and concedes that sometimes, because of past experience, we are very quick to jump to the interpretation. We do not need much repetition: if we are properly primed, just one example might impress itself on the mind, as when a child only has to burn itself once to be forewarned for the future. Similarly, he recognizes the complexity of causal fields, and the nice experiments in adding, subtracting, and varying factors before we can come to any grasp of their workings (T I.iii.15, pp. 173–5). He leaves room for more empirical psychology, such as work determining whether gaps in space and time diminish or extinguish our propensity to interpret sequences of happenings as causal.[16] But no such work affects the general outline of the theory, and in particular it leaves the crucial metaphysical conservatism perfectly intact.

The view brings *us* into the picture, clearly enough. And Hume knew that this was radical and surprising. He comments: 'I am sensible, that of all the paradoxes, which I have had, or shall hereafter have occasion to advance in the course of this treatise, the present one is the most violent' (T I.iii.14, p. 166). He imagines outraged common sense protesting: 'What! The efficacy of causes lie in the determination of the mind! As if causes did not operate entirely independent of the mind, and would not continue their operation, even tho' there was no mind existent to contemplate them, or reason concerning them' (T I.iii.14, p. 167).

But things are not so bad after all. Hume does not have to say, for instance, that were there no human beings about there would be no cases of one thing causing another to happen. Thus, suppose I imagine a world before human beings and I imagine in that world an iceberg in the sun, then I am also inclined to imagine it

So there is no sound "caused" by the fall of a tree if there is no one in the woods to hear it (or see it).

warming up and melting or disintegrating. This is a pattern I suppose to have held before we came on the scene, and that I expect to go on holding after we have left it. I can express my loyalty to it, as it were, by saying that of course the sun has always warmed and will continue to warm icebergs in its path, and as a result they will often melt or disintegrate. But I do not escape employing my own mind, shaped as it is by exposure to the patterns of events, as I say these things. (Similarly, I may say that some kind of world without people was good or beautiful or bad or nasty, thereby voicing my own passionate or sentimental take on how I imagine it to have been.) In the same way, Hume can talk of unknown and hidden causes, meaning that there are empirical patterns of events which we have not yet cottoned on to, either because of limited observations, or because of failures to register what are in fact repeatable patterns of things.

Some writers have contested Hume's apparently restrictive account of what we strictly observe, countering that in fact the causal relation between events is observable: we simply *see* people shoving and pushing, tugging and biffing, for instance. But Hume is right that a causal interpretation has consequences for more than the immediate scene. Causation throws its straitjacket over past and future. There is a close link, or even an identity, between causation (the impact of the ball shattered the glass) and counterfactuals (if the ball had not hit it, the glass would not have shattered). But we cannot observe counterfactuals to be true: we just see what is the case, not what would have been the case if something else had been different.

Another idea is that our causal interpretations somehow flow back to modify our actual visual or other experience. Seeing one event as causing another would then be different from seeing one merely following another. But this would just mean that the way we experience things has then been modified by the exposure to patterns of happenings that lie at the basis of our awareness. In allowing that, Hume need not concede that we observe anything metaphysically over and above the patterns of change he is happy to regard as the object of perception. Consider that perceiving a snake fearfully may be different from just perceiving a snake, but the difference does not lie in something additional being perceived. Likewise, perceiving a ball breaking a window (actually making a change) is different from simply perceiving a ball moving towards a window and the window shattering as it touches it. But if the difference consists in perceiving this sequence of events 'causally', as it were, Hume can be quite unperturbed. It is another functional change in the mind, but not our reception of a new kind of datum.

What about natural science? Doesn't it discover the causes of things? Well, yes and no. Yes, science discovers new patterns, new functional and mathematical relations, for instance between mass and velocity, or depth and pressure, or length of a pendulum and period of swing, and so on and so on. But as to the reasons underlying those patterns it brings to light, then in one sense, no. It can never show us why whatever *is* so *has to be* so. We are always dependent on the patterns that crop up. Beyond them we may find other more general patterns. But it is only ever more of the same. It is never the emergence of an illumination, a principle or insight with the status of a piece of pure logic or mathematics, which not only *does* but *must* issue in the kind of world we find around us. That kind of rational insight is forever denied us. It represents a dream or an illusion, a hope for a kind of security that the world is not going to afford us.

Losing this dream is painful. It is particularly so when we consider the ongoing order of nature: the fortunate fact that events do fall out the same across the most dizzying reaches of space and time. In our world, uniformity rules. But if we hope for any understanding of some fact or some 'thing', some kind of rule of law or marvellous time-proof straitjacket that explains this astonishing uniformity, we are doomed to disappointment. We have no idea of what we are looking for, and would not know it if we found it: 'we have no idea of this connexion, nor even any distinct notion what it is we desire to know, when we endeavour at a conception of it' (*E* 7, p. 146).

Does Hume, then, deny that there must be something that

explains, or would explain if only we could get hold of it, the ongoing uniformity of nature? Is he the equivalent of a dogmatic atheist about causation? No. He neither denies nor affirms it. Since we have no conception of what it could be, it does not signify whether we suppose such a 'thing' to exist or not. 'I am, indeed, ready to allow, that there may be several qualities both in material and immaterial objects, with which we are utterly unacquainted; and if we please to call these *power* or *efficacy*, it will be of little consequence to the world' (*T* I.iii.14, p. 168). As a consistent sceptic, Hume is happiest when he drives an issue beyond our understandings, so whether we find ourselves saying that there is, or is not, 'something there' does not matter in the least (we find exactly the same strategy in connection with God in chapter 9). Meanwhile, his modest picture of the human condition remains:

> It is confessed, that the utmost effort of human reason is to reduce the principles, productive of natural phenomena, to a greater simplicity, and to resolve the many particular effects into a few general causes, by means of reasonings from analogy, experience, and observation. But as to the causes of these general causes, we should in vain attempt their discovery; nor shall we ever be able to satisfy ourselves, by any particular explication of them. These ultimate springs and principles are totally shut up from human curiosity and enquiry . . . The most perfect philosophy of the natural kind only staves off our ignorance a little longer: as perhaps the most perfect philosophy of the moral or metaphysical kind serves only to discover larger portions of it. Thus the observation of human blindness and weakness is the result of all philosophy, and meets us at every turn, in spite of our endeavours to elude or avoid it. (*E* 4, pp. 111–12)

Hume shrank to vanishing point the way we can and cannot deploy ideas about causation in philosophical reasoning. Philosophers from Aristotle onwards had purported to show such general 'rational' or a priori principles as these: no activity of bare matter could give rise to mental events; no material world could exist without a cause; no bad thing could give rise to a better thing; human actions cannot be the result of antecedent circumstances; anything self-subsistent must be imperishable; motion can only arise from motion; causation must be a transfer of a quality in the cause to the same quality in the effect. Hume swept all this away. There are no a priori principles to be had. But he also showed the limitations on what can be gained even by empirical human inquiry. It has been fashionable lately to talk of the hope for a 'theory of everything'. Hume tells us that there cannot be such a thing, for every explanatory theory will need to rely on something that, as far as the theory itself can tell us, is no more than brute happenstance. There can only be a theory of things that are not taken for granted within the theory itself.

4

PERCEPTION AND THE EXTERNAL WORLD

Thus the sceptic still continues to reason and believe, even tho' he asserts, that he cannot defend his reason by reason; and by the same rule he must assent to the principle concerning the existence of body, tho' he cannot pretend by any arguments of philosophy to maintain its veracity. Nature has not left this to his choice, and has doubtless esteemed it an affair of too great importance to be trusted to our uncertain reasonings and speculations. We may well ask, *What causes induce us to believe in the existence of body?* but it is in vain to ask, *Whether there be body or not?* That is a point, which we must take for granted in all our reasonings.

T I.iv.2, p. 187

Perhaps the hardest chapter of the *Treatise* is book I, part iv, section 2: 'Of Scepticism with Regard to the Senses'. It is the section that above all attaches the label of scepticism to Hume. The distinguished commentator Jonathan Bennett, although holding that the discussion is 'a total failure', nevertheless allows that 'its depth and scope and disciplined complexity make it one of the most instructive arguments in modern philosophy'.[17] I don't agree about the total failure, but I do agree that, with the possible exception of Kant's *Critique of Pure Reason*, it is the deepest and most insightful treatment of perception in the modern period, at least until the later years of the twentieth century. The way to read it is first to understand thoroughly the problem space it is traversing.

The philosophical problem with perception can be put like this. It is perception that discloses the world to us. With perception we open ourselves to the world, or more particularly to the visible scene, or the layout of surrounding things showing visible properties (for brevity, I shall concentrate upon vision, although other senses must be borne in mind). But on the face of it our experience is one thing, and what we experience is another. For instance, our experience is under our own control; we can alter the direction of our gaze, and it can easily be shut off when we close our eyes. But the layout of surrounding objects stays the same. And a variety of common phenomena such as hallucinations, illusions, double vision, or the blurry appearance of things if we need spectacles but take them off, also lead us to recognize a distinction between how we are seeing things, and how they are.

Hume tends to concentrate on two features distinguishing experience from its objects. Our experiences are dependent upon us, whereas the layout of surrounding bodies is not, or not in the same way. And the layout is continuous, when experience is not. Bodies do not flicker in and out of existence as we close our eyes.

Hume is fairly brisk about arguing that our experiences, or 'perceptions', are dependent upon us, on 'our organs, and the disposition of our nerves and animal spirits' (T I.iv.2, p. 211). He cites the way in which we see double when we press upon an eyeball, but he clearly thinks it is obvious, and confirmed 'by an infinite number of other experiments of the same kind'. So, imagine a person in a rather unusual situation. He is facing a nicely illuminated egg, against a black background, which he sees perfectly normally. However, he shuts his eyes occasionally for short intervals, and then reopens them. It has been arranged that at some of these intervals, unknown to him, the egg will be substituted by a hologram of an egg, arranged to look indistinguishable from the original egg. And at other intervals a skilled neurophysiologist will stimulate electrodes that have been planted in his visual cortex to generate in a third way an indistinguishable visual experience, so that when he opens his eyes it will again be as if there is the illuminated egg against a black background, only in that case there will be no egg, nor a hologram of one. Let us call the sequence of these three situations, the Egg Sequence.

The subject's visual experience is indistinguishable whenever he opens his eyes, but the external layout of things is very different. Only in the one case is there an egg there. Yet since the cases are indistinguishable, from the subject's point of view, it is also natural to think of an identical visual experience, or 'perception' in Hume's terminology, produced in the three varying ways. After all, the subject cannot tell, just by looking, which of the three situations he is in. He knows how he is seeing things – as if there is an illuminated egg in front of him – but there are different ways the world might be, compatible with this being how it appears. Once we say this, however, the problem of perception opens up. It is by means of such experience that the world is disclosed to us. Yet how can experience have this power if, as just suggested, the same experience can coexist with widely different surrounding layouts of the world?

Perhaps the most obvious approach to this question is given by John Locke, but it is one of Hume's principal targets in the chapter.[18] Locke's view accepts a distinction between experience and reality, or postulates what Hume calls a 'double existence'. This view accepts that all that is given, subjectively, in a case like that of the egg, is the same indistinguishable visual experience. But it holds that on the basis of such experience we can *posit*, or adopt as a theory, an external, independent, relatively permanent world whose changes need not mirror the intermittent experiences of the subject. It is a coherent, relatively unchanging, and independent counterpart of that experience, which nevertheless adequately represents it. Provided this posit or theory is in good standing, the external world becomes the best explanation of the passing show, and deserves confidence accordingly. This view of the matter is still not uncommon among philosophers.

Yet it is subject to serious objections, so serious that Hume can say that Locke's story of double existence 'has no primary recommendation either to reason or the imagination' (*T* I.iv.2, p. 211). Amongst its problems are these. First, it seems to model our situation on that of an audience permanently stuck in a theatre, a 'sensorium' or inner space, in which experiences come and go, and then trying on that basis alone to make hypotheses about whatever it may be that lies outside the sensorium. It is not difficult to be sceptical about any 'theory' that is concocted. If one theorist says that things outside the inner theatre resemble those within, and another says that they do not, but only cause them, while a third says that there are no objects outside, but a deity or demon who wills the course of our experience, what could possibly settle the case? Furthermore, Hume's empiricism, already discussed, will forbid him any intelligible idea of things lying beyond the realm of experience. Our experiences are what they are. They cannot 'disclose', or make manifest, or enable us to look through them to, a different world altogether. In the story of a double existence, we are shut off from the world, and without even any idea of what it is that our experiences are supposed to represent. Furthermore, given Hume's picture of causation from the last chapter, we would be in no position to say that our experience is caused by something of a different kind unless we could, as it were, lift the veil of perception, and 'experience' both the experience itself *and* the world doing the causing. For Hume, since there are no a priori, non-experiential routes to causal knowledge, an interpretation of a sequence of events as causal requires access to both the antecedent, causing, event, and the subsequent effect. Our position would be analogous to trying to tell how well a portrait resembles a sitter, without access to both the portrait and the sitter. So, permanently stuck in a theatre, we cannot know what it is outside that causes the patterns of events unfolding within (in actual theatres we can know this, of course, but that is because we live mostly outside them).

Most modern philosophers endorse this, and many add that the supposed world of private experience cannot even be an object of thought. And since it could not be an object of thought, there can be no movement of the mind, no inference or act of making a posit to explain it, that launches us into the belief in the world of independent objects. This argument, which in chapter 2 was credited equally to Ludwig Wittgenstein and to Wilfrid Sellars, is not found in Hume, but it buttresses his total rejection of the Lockean picture. It is intended to show that any thought of our own experience can only be by way of concepts that have their primary application to things and their properties in the outside world. The subject in the Egg Sequence can think, 'Lo, an egg in front of me,' and he can also think, if he is aware of his situation, that perhaps it is not an egg, but that it only appears to him as if there is an egg in front of him. But even that thought requires a repertoire which starts with simple acceptance of there being, sometimes, eggs around and an ability to recognize them. Hence, there is no starting point, uncontaminated by thought of objects, that can afford the springboard to a theory that does embrace objects. This contrasts with the normal case of 'theoretical posits': in science, or history, the evidence is uncontroversially to hand, and can be accessed and identified antecedently to its theoretical interpretation. With experience and the external world, this is not so.

Locke's picture has no real grip on our imagination because it does not give us what we want from perception. We want the world to be visible to us. Our experience discloses it. It does not act as a surrogate for the world, or as a barrier, a kind of picture that substitutes itself for the external scene, getting in its way. Our experience is not the starting point of a piece of quasi-scientific theory, for experiencing how things stand enables us to dispense with theory. Our visual situation could not be what it is without carrying the indications of what it represents: to the hallucinating subject in the Egg Sequence it is always as if there is an egg there, and his experience is immediately saturated, as it were, with this interpretation. This is the way to say what the experience *is*. As Hume constantly insists, 'The very image, which is present to the senses, is with us the real body' (*T* I.iv.2, p. 205). Experience is, as it were, *transparent*. Just as we might look at the world outside our house through transparent windows of which we are seldom aware, so we look at it via transparent experience. Experience is not something getting in the way of an outside world, that therefore can only be guessed at. Its essence is to be revelatory.

Many of these objections to Locke were made before Hume, by Bishop George Berkeley, who also argued that Locke's 'double existence' led to complete scepticism, reducing the world as we experience it to a 'false imaginary glare'.[19] But Berkeley recoiled from Locke into an even less happy alternative: idealism. For Berkeley, it is experience all the way. There is no 'body' or matter. The world is as we represent it, but that means a world of ideas or experience, a world whose elements are themselves all mental items, presences in some mind. They fall into patterns, right enough, enabling us to predict and act. But in the entire world, there is nothing else. Hume admits Berkeley's arguments, but simply dismisses his conclusion as unbelievable. We do believe in 'body'. Furthermore, we have to do so. Nature is too strong for us.

But now the trap is sprung. On the one hand, we have to do justice to the phenomena, here illustrated by the subject in the Egg Sequence, that force us to distinguish experience and its normal object, the 'body', which in this case is the actual egg. On the other hand, we cannot tolerate the theory to which this leads, the story of the double existence. But we cannot put up with anything else either, since the only theory of 'single existence' on hand is the intolerable Berkeley.

This, then, is the ground Hume traverses, with consummate skill. The upshot is a catastrophe: nature forces us to believe something that the least reflection shows us *cannot possibly be true*. It forces us to hold that the perceptions which we know to be dependent (on ourselves), and discontinuous, are at the same time *identical with* the independent and continuous objects of the external world. We are revealed as holding that our perceptions or experiences *themselves* 'continue identically and uninterruptedly the same in all their interrupted appearances' (*T* I.iv.2, p. 216). We know, as soon as we reflect, that they do not. But we are condemned to talk and think and act on the supposition that they do.

This is not so much a theory about the relation between experience and its objects as a view of how we get by when there is no coherent theory to hand. Hume is perfectly clear about this:

This sceptical doubt, both with respect to reason and the senses, is a malady, which can never be radically cured, but must return

> upon us every moment, however we may chase it away, and some-
> times may seem entirely free from it. It is impossible upon any
> system to defend either our understanding or senses; and we but
> expose them farther when we endeavour to justify them in that
> manner. As the sceptical doubt arises naturally from a profound
> and intense reflection on those subjects, it always encreases, the
> farther we carry our reflections, whether in opposition or con-
> formity to it. Carelessness and in-attention alone can afford us
> any remedy. For this reason I rely entirely upon them; and take it
> for granted, whatever may be the reader's opinion at this present
> moment, that an hour hence he will be persuaded there is both
> an external and internal world. (*T* I.iv.2, p. 218)

The situation here is much worse than it is with induction and
causation. There we have aspects of our nature that cannot be 'certified' by reason. We go in for inferences that cannot be shown to
be probable. But here, right at the heart of our entire conception
of ourselves and our world, we go in for beliefs that can be shown
not only to be improbable, but to be straightforwardly contradictory. We cannot help it, and we cannot mend it either:
'carelessness and inattention alone can afford us any remedy'.

The situation is also worse than in previous philosophies, also
regarded as 'sceptical'. So-called Cartesian scepticism takes off
from Descartes's fear that all his experience might be the product
of the *malin genie*: the evil demon that feeds him nothing but a diet
of hallucination and illusion. Rejecting Descartes's own attempt to
show that it is not like that by means of dubious proofs of a good,
and therefore not a deceiving, deity, Cartesian scepticism concludes that we cannot rule out the hypothesis of the evil demon,
and therefore do not know that we are located in an external
world of independent objects. This may or may not worry us: the
hypothesis of the evil demon is after all sufficiently far-fetched for
us to live our lives ignoring it. But Hume leaves us much worse
off. Cartesian scepticism says that things are just *possibly* not as we
take them to be. Hume says that things *cannot* be as we take them
to be. We are not condemned to insecurity, but to falsehood.

Similarly ancient, classical scepticism tried to convince us that in important theoretical matters there was always a balance of opinion, equally strong arguments pulling in opposite directions, so that the only wise course was to avoid positive commitment and to suspend judgement. This too is relatively anodyne by comparison. To Hume, there are not equally strong arguments pulling in opposite directions. The voice of argument points in one direction only. It points unambiguously and unanswerably to the falsity of our everyday conception of the world and our place in it.

Hume's achievement in this section will be less impressive if we think there is an easy way out, a third way between Locke and Berkeley, perhaps undermining some concealed assumption that is structuring the whole way the problem appears. Many modern authors have supposed that there is, and that it is relatively easy to overcome the problem, to dismantle the thoughts on which it depends.

Ironically, some suggestions amount to little more than emphasizing the transparency of experience. But as we have seen, this is a central part of Hume's own armoury. It is the reason why we must reject the hypothesis of double existence: 'the very image, which is present to the senses, is with us the real body'. Announcing the phenomenon of transparency as if by itself it solved the problem is simply taking up one half of the problem. The other half, which says that this can't possibly be so, is simply ignored.

A better proposal is that the mistake lies in the very noun 'experience' or the very idea of 'perceptions' as Hume discusses them. Macbeth asks, 'Is this a dagger which I see before me, the handle toward my hand?' and has a perfectly good question. Similarly the subject in the Egg Sequence may ask whether *this* is an egg or a mere hallucination. It sounds as though the word 'this' refers at any rate to *something*. This thought tempts us to treat experiences as 'things' – and then these things must either be identical with external things (heavy? expensive? sharp?) or they must be other things entirely, and each suggestion is untenable. But suppose we have been misled by grammar, and can reject the image forced on us by this treatment? We might suggest instead that we are dealing with processes of perception, or states of a subject rather than things in some kind of private space. And then the metaphor of the 'inner theatre' collapses, and perhaps we can struggle towards a much better model than the one that Hume shared with other early modern philosophers. Hume's attachment to the 'thinginess' of his perceptions is undeniable: as we shall see again in the next chapter, he even thinks it possible that individual perceptual experiences should exist on their own, without belonging to any mind. Whereas if we think in terms of states of individuals, this is not so: an experiential state could no more exist independently of a subject than a dent could exist without a surface to be dented.

Perhaps this begins to solve the problem. But it is not plain sailing. We may try to think of visual states as states that do not involve a 'this', which then might or might not be an egg or a dagger. The problem remains that the Egg Sequence and similar phenomena still suggest that there is a division between such states, however we think of them, and the state of the world. There is a gap between 'what we have to go on' and what we believe. If, as Hume suggests, we have inconsistent attitudes to that gap, sometimes treating it as closed (transparency) and sometimes treating it as open (when we reflect on the dependent nature of our visual states), then our situation is as bad as he says it is, whether or not we treat experiences as things in a private, subjective space.

Some philosophers take a different tack. They suggest that there is nothing interesting in common between the three indistinguishable phases of the Egg Sequence. When the egg is there and is seen, the subject is in one state: seeing an egg. When nothing is there, he is in a different state: hallucinating an egg. In the hologram phase, he is in a different state again: seeing a hologram, not an egg. If we 'type' visual states in terms of their objects, we can wean ourselves away from the idea that there is anything important to the philosophy of perception that is common to all three phases. And that opens the way to exorcizing all the problems by which Hume is beset.[20]

This has recently been a popular line, but it is not on the face of it all that promising. We can type visual states in terms of objects, certainly. We can say that seeing an egg is a different visual experience from hallucinating one. But there is certainly *something* in common between all three phases of the Egg Sequence. In each of them things look the same, indistinguishable. It looks to the subject as if there is an egg before him. And it seems impossible to deny that how things look, or otherwise appear, is of primary epistemological importance. How things look had better afford excellent evidence of how they are. So we still face the question of how this is so. If our only way of answering that is by sometimes equating how things look and how they are, and then when the going gets difficult, remembering to distinguish them, then our situation is once more in danger of inconsistency, just as Hume claims.

A better kind of approach, I believe, would be to stay relaxed about the identity of the experience in the three phases of the Egg Sequence, but to insist on the primacy of the veridical case in a different way. The proper function of the visual system is to enable us to know how things stand. It makes us into good instruments for detecting eggs, their position in relation to us, and their visible properties. It is no problem that it is sometimes fooled, any more than it is a problem that a digestive system adapted to break down sugar might be fooled into treating some non-sugar as sugar, or even into churning away when there is nothing to digest, because it has been stimulated by the scientist with his electrodes. We do not have to say that the churning is different in these three different cases. Vision's success lies in its selecting for us the features that we need in order to navigate our way around our environment. We are overwhelmingly successful at doing that (just try to do the same without employing vision, or the other senses). It is only when we conceptualize 'visual experience' and 'the way things are' in terms of either parallel or identical 'spaces', inner and outer, that we cannot make a consistent story about how vision works. It would be nice if we could see how to reflect and reason on the process without entrapping ourselves in such an image, but even now the large and controversial literature on the topic proves that it will not be easy.

Hume's discussion of all this comes in the last part of book I of the *Treatise*, and corresponding, but somewhat more muted, passages come at the end of the *Enquiry Concerning Human Understanding*. He does not, of course, deny himself the right to go on thinking and talking in terms of the external world, and all his writings from these points coincide with common sense in taking that for granted. But the despondent result of the investigation is not forgotten. It stands in Hume's mind as a monument to the failure of reason. It shows that if we push our researches too far, we are likely, even on such a familiar issue, to end up in confusion and contradiction. So it clips the wings of theory, reminding us that even in the most humdrum and everyday matters, natural belief is paramount.

5

PERSONAL IDENTITY AND THE SELF

For my part, when I enter most intimately into what I call *myself*, I always stumble on some particular perception or other, of heat or cold, light or shade, love or hatred, pain or pleasure. I never can catch *myself* at any time without a perception, and never can observe any thing but the perception. When my perceptions are removed for any time, as by sound sleep; so long am I insensible of *myself*, and may truly be said not to exist. And were all my perceptions removed by death, and could I neither think, nor feel, nor see, nor love, nor hate after the dissolution of my body, I should be entirely annihilated, nor do I conceive what is farther requisite to make me a perfect non-entity. If any one, upon serious and unprejudiced reflection, thinks he has a different notion of *himself*, I must confess I can reason no longer with him. All I can allow him is, that he may be in the right as well as I, and that we are essentially different in this particular. He may, perhaps, perceive something simple and continued, which he calls *himself*; tho' I am certain there is no such principle in me.

T I.iv.6, p. 252

This passage expresses Hume's difficulty with the idea of an enduring self, a subject which enjoys diverse perceptions, the possessor of experience and passion, the agent that wills and thinks and plans. In the light of the empiricist principle governing impressions and ideas, his question is whether we have an 'impression' that can authenticate any such idea, and Hume's resounding conclusion is that we do not. We certainly *seem* to ourselves to mean something quite definite when we expect ourselves to do things, or expect events to happen to us. It is not the same as expecting a thing to be done, but only by someone or other, or expecting an event to happen to someone, who may or may not be us ourselves. Hume considers our propensity to think like this to be some kind of result of an imagination, a matter of conniving at a fiction. Our perceptions are connected, he believes, by relations of resemblance and continuity, and by causation. Our trains of thought, experience, and passion are not 'invariable and uninterrupted', but in imagination we somehow smooth over the changes, and relax into the fiction of an uninterrupted and perfect identity underlying them. The shifting scenes, we convince ourselves, take place in the one identical theatre.

The metaphysical problem of personal identity through time is usually put like this. I live the life of an animal, with all the growth, change, and decay inherent in that life. I am scarcely at all like the little boy I once was, either physically or mentally. What, then, if anything, makes it true that I am *the same person* as him? What is the 'unity relation' that holds together the successive stages of my life as the life of one person? In the century before Hume, John Locke had asked this question, and decided that two possible answers wouldn't do.[21] It was useless to appeal to an unchanging 'substance', a kind of soul or soul stuff, a nugget of unchanging *me* continuing serenely underneath the bodily and mental kaleidoscope. For might not my consciousness continue, although the metaphysical substance changed? Perhaps God changes the metaphysical substance on a daily basis, but I myself soldier on. In other words, there are no principles connecting the identity of this 'substance' with what I experience and remember. And although it was better, it was still insufficient to cite animal continuity, the mere biological continuation of the one, changing animal. For we could imagine this one animal that I am, taken over by a different subject. My brain might be reprogrammed into being the mouthpiece on earth of the mad cosmic scientist. And then it would no longer be *me*. Because of this possibility, Locke concluded, the answer had to lie in the continued consciousness of past doings and experiences. That would be ruptured by the takeover and reprogramming, but so long as such a thing does not happen, then there is a chain of memory uniting me with the doings of a predecessor, and we are the same person. Personal identity lies in a relation between present and past states of mind.

True to his general orientation, Hume is not centrally bothered by the metaphysical question. He is bothered about how we think about personal identity, rather than what it is. It is the way our imagination works rather than the way the world works that interests him. But he agrees with Locke that the key to the way we think of ourselves lies in the way the associative tendencies of the mind work on the train of perceptions that makes up our conscious life. There is a strong parallel between the 'imperfect identity' of things and persons: in each case associative principles of resemblance, contiguity, or causation lead us to overlook difference and substitute a fictional identity.

Hume condensed and reviewed his thoughts about the self and its identity in the Appendix to the *Treatise*, written within two years of his completion of book I, in which the original discussion appeared. In the short version in the Appendix, he starts from the premise that every idea is derived from a preceding impression, but that we have no impression of self or substance, as something 'simple and individual'. We have, therefore 'no idea of them in that sense'. He then asserts that all our perceptions are distinguishable, and therefore can be conceived as 'separable', as enjoying an independent, solitary existence. He points out that this is how we think of tables and chimneys, so there is no a priori difficulty in applying it to perceptions; as we have already seen, Hume is inclined to downplay the difference between ordinary things in space and perceptions, since we vulgarly think of them as identical in any event.

Hume next asks us to think of a mind 'reduced even below the life of an oyster', possessing perhaps one perception, as of thirst or hunger. 'Do you conceive any thing but merely that perception? Have you any notion of *self* or *substance*?' And if this is true of such a simple life, 'the addition of other perceptions can never give you that notion' (*T* Appendix, p. 634).

This is the negative phase. But then Hume wants to 'explain the principle of connexion' which binds perceptions together 'and makes us attribute to them a real simplicity and identity'. He reminds himself of the principle that 'no connexions among distinct existences are ever discoverable by human understanding. We only feel a connexion or determination of the thought, to pass from one object to another.' But this is all in order, since when we reflect on our own experiences, the ideas of them are 'felt to be connected together, and naturally introduce each other'. It is quite parallel, here, to the philosophy of causation where, as we saw in chapter 3, the mind's inability to discover a real causal connection between distinct events is made up for by our natural propensities to infer and predict. So far, so good: 'the present philosophy, therefore, has so far a promising aspect' (*T* Appendix, p. 635).

But then there comes a bombshell. Hume's hopes suddenly vanish, he throws in the towel, and confesses to total defeat, to an inconsistency in his principles, to some insuperable problem, a labyrinth with no way out that he can see:

> In short there are two principles, which I cannot render consistent; nor is it in my power to renounce either of them, viz. *that all our distinct perceptions are distinct existences*, and *that the mind never perceives any real connexion among distinct existences*. Did our perceptions either inhere in something simple and individual, or did the mind perceive some real connexion among them, there would be no difficulty in the case. For my part, I must plead the privilege of a sceptic, and confess, that this difficulty is too hard for my understanding. I pretend not, however, to pronounce it absolutely insuperable. Others, perhaps, or myself, upon more mature reflexions, may discover some hypothesis, that will reconcile those contradictions. (*T* Appendix, p. 636)

The question this leaves for interpreters of Hume is: what was the bombshell he thought he had discovered? This is the only part of his serious metaphysics and epistemology about which Hume ever showed this kind of hesitation, and must be something pretty horrendous, repeatedly said to engender 'inconsistency' and 'contradiction'. But what is the difficulty?

Whatever the problem is, Hume underdescribes it, since the two principles he italicizes are not contradictory, and throughout book I of the *Treatise*, Hume had applied them each of them quite happily. Nor is there any evidence that he abandoned either of them when he came to write the *Enquiry*. Although the later work is notably silent about personal identity, Hume says in a letter that the 'philosophical principles are the same' in both the *Treatise* and the first *Enquiry* (although he also said that he wished later critics would take the *Enquiry* as his last word, rather than the *Treatise*).[22] Furthermore, in spite of the despairing tone of this part of the Appendix, Hume did not seem particularly distressed by his confession. In the subsequent books of the *Treatise*, he talks of the self constantly, discussing the passionate self, or self-love and self-interest, without any embarrassment. Whatever the problem was, he evidently felt that he could quarantine it.

There are dozens of different suggestions that various commentators have made about his problem. Some think that the kind of fiction he is positing will not do the work of supporting the subsequent discussions of the self in the work on the passions. But this seems unlikely, partly because it does not support the talk of contradiction, and partly because it is only the aspects of our thought that issue in the idea of a self with 'perfect identity and simplicity' (*T* I.iv.6, p. 251), or a self that is 'simple and continued' (*T* I.iv.6, p. 252), or 'invariable and uninterrupted' (*T* I.iv.6, p. 253), that are his target in the discussion, and these are not the thoughts in play when we are motivated by thoughts about ourselves, for instance in acting because of greed or self-interest or pride. Some think that the failure is to explain how there is an active mind, a subject that wills and controls and does things. But this is an explanatory gap rather than a contradiction, and in any case it is not very likely that Hume would be perturbed by it, since the whole tendency of his science of human nature is to substitute happenings for doings, or in other words to explain what we do in terms of what we find ourselves doing, which means: what we find happening in our minds.

In Hume's system, the connection between perceptions is contingent, like that of stars that happen to form constellations, but could equally have existed without doing so. So some think that Hume had stumbled on the problem that his system permits unowned perceptions, whereas it is plausibly thought to be necessarily true that if there exists a pain, for instance, then there exists a subject whose pain it is. But, rightly or wrongly, Hume continued to assert the contrary quite blithely even in the Appendix. It is the moral of the discussion of the mind 'reduced even below the life of an oyster'. As we saw in the last chapter, it is true that if he had started to take this problem seriously, Hume might have needed to unravel a good deal of his philosophy of mind, thinking less in terms of perceptions as kinds of object, and more in terms of subjects and their modifications. But there is no independent evidence that he ever did take it seriously.

Some think Hume realized that he could not explain the principles of association of ideas that create the mechanisms of imagination. But generally speaking Hume is perfectly happy with explanations that rest on things that are not themselves explained, for as we have seen, these are always the endpoint of the sciences ('the most perfect philosophy of the natural kind only staves off our ignorance a little longer', quoted in chapter 3). Others suggest that Hume cannot integrate the ideas we have when we reflect on our own perceptions (what he calls secondary ideas: T I.i.1, p. 6; T I.iii.9, p. 106) with primary perceptions as their objects. It is as if we are rather literally in two minds – the one that is made up of primary perceptions, mostly experiences of the world around us, and the other constituted by our secondary reflections on those original perceptions. Yet, insofar as causation and resemblance do any work, they would seem to work here as well: our reflections on our own experience certainly seem to 'resemble' our experiences just as much as ideas ever resemble impressions, and they also seem to be caused by them. I would not, for instance, be reflecting on my joyous experience of seeing the Taj Mahal, had I not seen it in the first place.

A popular suggestion or family of suggestions is that it is the 'string around the bundle' that Hume cannot really explain. That is, if we imagine a universe of 'perceptions' floating around, quite unsorted into subjects, quite unattached, then 'resemblance' and 'causation' will not do the job of sorting them into bundles of individual 'minds'. For why shouldn't an experience of mine resemble one of yours (we often suppose they do), or a memory in my mind trigger one in yours?

This is certainly a more serious problem. And Hume is in no position to invoke spatial position, contiguity, as a supplementary principle, since he explicitly denies that 'contiguity', his other principle of association, has anything to offer in the case of personal identity (T I.iv.6, p. 260). We could not bundle these unattached perceptions by means of where they occur, since they have no location, he thinks. But there is something uncomfortable about this interpretation as well. The main problem is that it arises from a highly 'metaphysical' point of view, the position of a God, as it were, to whom all perceptions are 'given', and who then has the sorting problem. This is emphatically not the starting point in which any of us find ourselves; on the contrary, all that is 'given' to us is a small subset of all perceptions, namely our own, and the sorting problem never arises for us. So it is highly unlikely that Hume would be particularly despondent if the sorting problem proved insoluble for an imaginary being who did face it. His quest was to find the mechanism of mind responsible for us thinking in terms of an identical self, something that preserves its identity through change, when all that we can ever catch, when we attempt to gain an impression of this self, are the experiences of the moment.

To me it seems unlikely that there is one determinate, defensible answer to what had so rocked Hume in the Appendix. There is, however, a great deal more to say about the role that reference to a self or subject of experience plays in our thinking.[23] And this makes it tempting, if speculative, to think that Hume had glimpsed something of these future developments. For instance, in the quotation at the head of the chapter, he makes it sound as though it would be easy to understand the self if experience revealed something unchanging alongside the changing scenes of life, the stable theatre within which the scenes unfold, as it were. But it is easy to argue that this is a mistake. The thought of myself as a subject of experience would not be any easier to understand if I became acquainted with some unchanging element of my experience. The thought that *I* am hearing some music would not be any more intelligible if in addition to the music I always heard the same background drone. *That* would just give me two things to think about: that I am hearing the music, and that I am hearing the drone. Similarly for any of the other senses. My awareness that at long last I have seen the Northern Lights would not be easier to comprehend if in addition to the flickering lights there was a fixed blob of some kind in the corner of the scene.

Yet it is also hard to see Hume as subliminally aware of future developments. When he has unveiled the contradiction in the Appendix, Hume writes: 'Did our perceptions either inhere in something simple or individual, or did the mind perceive some real connexion among them, there would be no difficulty in the case' (*T* Appendix, p. 636). He has little right to say either of these things. He has argued long and effectively that the idea of a perception 'inhering in something simple or individual' makes no sense, and neither does the idea of a perceptible real connexion. So neither can make up an intelligible hypothesis, such that if we supposed it true, some current difficulty would disappear.

Perhaps the most charitable course is to credit Hume with some dim awareness that a wholly different approach from his sensory empiricism is needed in order to deal with the concept of the subject of experience. Perhaps at some level he realizes something of what Kant would subsequently put in the centre of the picture: that the concept of the self is a formal or structural concept, rather than an empirical one. It is not something recognized or identified in experience, nor a construction or fiction generated by the imagination, but is instead a necessary accompaniment to our ability to synthesize or construct any kind of picture of a world, and any kind of thought at all. In a famous passage, Kant wrote:

> It must be possible for the 'I think' to accompany all my repre-sentations; for otherwise something would be represented in me which could not be thought at all, and that is equivalent to saying that the representation would be impossible, or at least would be nothing to me.[24]

Kant recognizes that it must be possible for me to become con-scious of any of my experiences at all as 'mine', for anything of which this was not possible 'would be nothing to me'. But that in turn implies that 'self-consciousness', the bringing of myself into my thoughts, is not an extra grasped by intruding another element into a scene (one which might not originally have been there). It is rather a way of distributing attention, or synthesizing together an experience and a life, and not a question of *what* we apprehend so much as *how* we apprehend in the first place. But in turn, doing anything with that pregnant idea would require a leap beyond Hume's empiricism about the elements of thought. It would require seeing that 'I' has more a logical function than a represen-tational one: it needs a theory more like one appropriate to terms such as 'and' or 'not', words which organize our thoughts and whose meaning is given by that role, rather than one appropriate to terms like 'red' or 'hard', given by what they represent.

Hume's problem with the simple, unified self is echoed as loudly as any of his other ideas in our own time. Writers and philosophers are familiar with the idea that the self is an illusion, that it is a 'construct' or fiction arising from the need to try to grasp and comprehend experience, or that we are at best a rag-bag of forces and processes whose natures we see only dimly. This is often thought to be a peculiarly modern idea, to be credited per-haps to Freud, or perhaps to Nietzsche:

> What separates me most deeply from metaphysicians is: I don't concede that the 'I' is what thinks. Instead, I take the I itself to

be a construction of thinking . . . in other words to be only a *regulative fiction* with the help of which a kind of constancy, and thus 'knowability' is inserted into, *invented into*, a world of becoming.[25]

But Hume was there beforehand, both with the idea and with the difficulty of coming to terms with it.

With this we end our discussion of Hume's fundamental treatment of human understanding. He draws this part of the *Treatise* to a close with a rhetorical cry of despair, a self-dramatizing display of scepticism and melancholy. When he recast his philosophy in the first *Enquiry*, the melancholy is downplayed, and relegated to the kind of thing you might expect if you push philosophical inquiry beyond the limited extent to which reason can support it. But in both works, the empiricism, the theory of causation, the doctrine of the priority of natural belief over reason, and the background of 'mitigated scepticism' are never forgotten. They continue to operate in the *Treatise* and both *Enquiries* as Hume turns to the more practical, less sceptical, more constructive side of his philosophy, his account of our motivations, our passions, and our place in the social world.

6

THE PRINCIPLES OF MORALS

We speak not strictly and philosophically when we talk of the combat of passion and of reason. Reason is, and ought only to be the slave of the passions, and can never pretend to any other office than to serve and obey them . . . Where a passion is neither founded on false suppositions, nor chuses means insufficient for the end, the understanding can neither justify nor condemn it. It is not contrary to reason to prefer the destruction of the whole world to the scratching of my finger. It is not contrary to reason for me to chuse my total ruin, to prevent the least uneasiness of an *Indian* or person wholly unknown to me. It is as little contrary to reason to prefer even my own acknowledged lesser good to my greater, and have a more ardent affection for the former than the latter . . . In short, a passion must be accompanyed with some false judgment in order to its being unreasonable; and even then it is not the passion, properly speaking, which is unreasonable, but the judgment.

T II.iii.3, pp. 415–16

'Passion' is Hume's general term for emotion, attitude, and desire. He gives two lists of what he has in mind. There are direct passions, which include 'desire, aversion, grief, joy, hope, fear, despair and security'. And there are indirect passions, which include 'pride, humility, ambition, vanity, love, hatred, envy, pity, malice, generosity, with their dependants' (*T* II.i.1, pp. 276–7). The difference need not overly concern us: roughly, while desire and aversion are related to their objects quite simply, the indirect passions bring in more complexity. Pride, for example, requires us not only to be pleased about something, but also to relate whatever it is to ourselves in some way. We should note at the outset that his term 'passion' by no means equates with the modern term 'emotion'. A desire or aversion could be quite unemotional. They do not even name episodes in our conscious lives, since they are more in the nature of dispositions, background tendencies that will prompt us to feel things and do things only on occasion. They may lay us open to emotional occurrences when they are gratified or thwarted, but that would be a different matter. If I am angry at having my desire for revenge on someone thwarted, the emotion is the anger, not the desire for revenge itself.

His account of the passions shows Hume at his most joyfully radical, for his view of reason as the slave of the passions inverts the philosophical hierarchy that had held from Plato and Aristotle to his own day, in which one of the glorious offices of reason was to direct and channel, encourage, or more often to suppress whatever dangerous and undisciplined desires emerged from the lawless, boiling cauldron of human passion.

Hume holds that both reason and passion are necessary for motivation. We must place ourselves in some context in order to act. We must see how things stand, and this is the work of understanding the world. But that only sets the stage for passion to do its work, giving us either an aversion to or pain at what we find, which motivates us to change it; or a delight or pleasure, which motivates us to pursue it. In the absence of the passions, what we find would be of no interest to us one way or the other, but would lie dead and inert. So the office of cognition is to set the stage for action. But it does so only by serving the passions with materials which excite them.

Hume has a simple argument that 'passions' are not themselves discovered by reason, nor in themselves subject to its verdicts:

A passion is an original existence, or, if you will, modification of existence, and contains not any representative quality, which

renders it a copy of any other existence or modification. When I
am angry, I am actually possest with the passion, and in that
emotion have no more a reference to any other object, than when
I am thirsty, or sick, or more than five foot high. It is impossible,
therefore, that this passion can be opposed by, or be contradictory to truth and reason; since this contradiction consists in the
disagreement of ideas, considered as copies, with those objects,
which they represent. (*T* II.iii.3, p. 415)

There is a wrong way to read this. It might seem as if Hume is
denying that emotions 'have reference to' any objects, to which it
may baldly be replied that they do. If I am angry at you for insult-
ing me, the anger is directed at your insult, and this is typical of
emotions: I may be afraid of the bull in the field, or depressed at
the morning news. In the jargon, emotions and desires are 'inten-
tional' states, directed at real or supposed facts, actions, or events.
Hume should not be read as denying that. Instead he is asserting
that the *specific* nature of passion, the particular way it directs
thought and action, is not itself determined solely by what is
thought to be the case. I might find you have insulted me, and be
angry, or I might think of it as merely comical, or regard it with
contempt, or I might even take pride in being insulted by someone as dreadful as you. I may or may not feel angry about it. All
these specific emotions and attitudes are not mere registrations of
what is found, but personal, variable, and active reactions to it.
The bull in the field that terrifies you into fleeing may leave sto-
ical me calm and unperturbed, while it motivates some macho
third party to go and play the fool with it.

This should help to fend off another way of misunderstanding
the idea that reason connects with action only by serving the passions with materials which excite them. One may complain that
Hume, the great opponent of armchair, a priori theorizing about
what can cause what, has no business denying that the occurrence
of a perception or belief could cause anything at all – including an
action, just like that. And after all, it is familiar enough that this
happens. The perception of a snake, in itself just a cognitive

change, makes me jump backwards, just as it makes my heart race or stomach constrict. Such causal relations may be quite automatic. But Hume should not be read as if he is somehow (amazingly) blind to that kind of fact. His point is rather that being the sort of person who implements this causal pattern, that is, someone in whom the perception of a snake causes those effects, is just what it is to be afraid of snakes. The passion is attributed exactly on that kind of basis. If, being an experienced herpetologist, you react with a whoop of joy and by picking the creature up, then you are someone who has no fear of snakes, but instead has a fascination with them.

This in turn has invited the hostile reply that if that is his point, Hume would be turning his claim into a pure matter of definition. Of course motivation requires passion, if whenever someone becomes motivated as the result of a belief, that is enough to diagnose them as having a passion. The theory may seem no more than a verbal trick. But in turn that ignores the way in which theories work. Consider a parallel objection to Newton. 'Look,' someone might say, 'it is merely a verbal trick to say that force is proportional to mass times acceleration, if whenever a body accelerates we simply proclaim a force or combination of forces acting on it.' The reason that objection is no good is that there are other things to say about force, mass, and acceleration as well. The axiom takes its place as one piece of a whole theory – and that whole theory is not at all 'merely verbal', but one of the most fertile and successful in the whole of empirical science. Similarly, the instruction to diagnose the operation of a passion whenever a perception or other belief results in a behaviour or change in behaviour is part of an overall theory, 'folk psychology', which enables us to find constancies and make predictions about the behaviour of others.

Thus, it is a good bet that the person we diagnosed as afraid of snakes will show parallel symptoms on other occasions. He will be disinclined to fossick around in rubbish heaps in India, or stick his hand into piles of logs in the American south. It might be a bad idea to put him in charge of a night patrol in the jungle, and so on. Knowing that you desire to catch a flight enables me to predict and understand a whole variety of your doings, from setting an alarm, to finding your passport, to ordering a taxi, and all the rest. The desire is an 'intervening variable', a theoretical construction or description of a fact about persons that can be deployed in countless circumstances to anticipate what to expect, or to instruct us on how to control or react to them.

With these misunderstandings out of the way, Hume's view might seem no more than simple common sense, and in a way it is. It is echoed, for instance, in modern subjects such as decision theory or game theory, which also work in terms of a pairing of belief and desire. The need for a pair of mental states to work together is often put in terms of their opposite 'direction of fit' with the world. The job of belief is to fit the world, to represent it as it is. The job of desire or passion is to get the world to fit it: in other words, it is to activate the subject to change things so that the desire is satisfied. Action requires both. Cognition without passion would be inert, and passion without cognition would be at sea. A belief is an opportunity for a desire to become practical; a desire gives a belief an opportunity to become practical.

Hume of course knows that we do talk of reason overcoming passion, and there are the undeniable phenomena of practical reasoning: thinking things through, taking a long-term view, seeking accommodations with others, performing cost-benefit calculations, and so forth. He interprets them in terms of, first, finding out more about the situation, and second, comparing and balancing different kinds of concern. So admitting that 'it is seldom men heartily love what lies at a distance from them, and what no way redounds to their particular benefit', he makes room for a tussle between 'general calm determination of the passions, founded on some distant view or reflexion' and the more impetuous, short-term, and selfish passions which are so apt to lead us by the nose (T III.iii.1, p. 583). When we try to control ourselves, we are in fact balancing one kind of concern against another. It is often a toss-up whether we listen to the voice of prudence, accommodate others, take up a 'common point of view', or let ourselves stray down the primrose path of temptation.

And so we come to ethics. Hume's point of entry is character-istically one of down-to-earth empirical observation of human nature as we find it. So he comes at it by considering things that we admire about people, or dislike about them, which are equally things we would like hearing said about ourselves, as opposed to things we would be mortified to hear or would regard as imputa-tions which we would wish to refute. Hume thinks that even if you are weary of the sound of morality, you cannot escape these passions, or attitudes:

> In like manner I find, that, of old, the perpetual cant of the STOICS and CYNICS concerning *virtue*, their magnificent professions and slender performances, bred a disgust in mankind; and LUCIAN, who, though licentious with regard to pleasure, is yet, in other respects, a very moral writer, cannot, sometimes, talk of virtue, so much boasted, without betraying symptoms of spleen and irony. But surely this peevish delicacy, whence-ever it arises, can never be carried so far as to make us deny the existence of every species of merit, and all distinction of manners and behaviour. Besides *discretion, caution, enterprise, industry, assiduity, fru-gality, œconomy, good-sense, prudence, discernment*; besides these endowments, I say, whose very names force an avowal of their merit, there are many others, to which the most determined scepticism cannot, for a moment, refuse the tribute of praise and approbation. *Temperance, sobriety, patience, constancy, perse-verance, forethought, considerateness, secrecy, order, insinuation, address, presence of mind, quickness of conception, facility of expression*; these, and a thousand more of the same kind, no man will ever deny to be excellencies and perfections. (*EM* 6.21, pp. 125–6)

I like to offer this passage to anyone impressed by the posture of suspicion of ethics, as found in Nietzsche or his existentialist fol-lowers, or any self-proclaimed 'amoralist' sneering at the social world from exile in Bohemia. Indeed, Hume thought that a great deal of ethics, and any worthwhile 'general precepts', were implicit in everyday language. Anyone who understands a natural language knows which terms carry commendations with them, and which carry criticism. And we cannot escape assessing others, and being ourselves assessed, in these terms. Even the misanthropic exile is likely to derive more pleasure from being considered perceptive and thoughtful than selfish and ignorant. Of course, Hume is also aware that history can shift the aspects which are more important at particular times: martial societies will admire the 'rough heroes' of Homer; courtly societies will prize the softer and more sociable virtues, and so on.

Our appreciation of character is not primarily selfish. It does not depend on the benefit the person in question brings to us. We can applaud or deplore a historical character who isn't going to do us any good or any harm. Indeed, a great deal of moral education is conducted through fiction, where no actual person is involved at all. What we do is take up the point of view of those who were, either in reality or fiction, directly affected by the character: the family or friends or those playing on his team, as it were. A social virtue, such as benevolence, is then a trait which would have done them good, and ourselves feeling that, we admire the subject for it. The mechanism here is one of sympathy or empathy, initiated, however, by an exercise of imagination: feeling for ourselves what it *would* be like to be thrown in with this character, we recognize the pleasure it could have brought, if it is virtuous, or the trouble and pain it would have brought, if it is vicious. And 'internalizing' those outcomes, we admire or despise accordingly.

As well as social traits, however, Hume thinks there are qualities of mind that serve the subject himself, and he realizes that we admire those as well. A person's perseverance or dedication to a task, or his spirit or dignity, may be qualities which mostly serve himself, yet they too are admirable. Furthermore, agreeable qualities, as well as useful ones, excite our admiration: gaiety, serenity, tranquillity, as well as personal beauty and grace, attract us and generate love and admiration. Some say that these are more in the nature of talents than anything to do with ethics. But Hume acknowledges no interesting distinction between talents in general and virtues in particular. We try to avoid the blockhead or the bigot or the cheerless just as we do the person of ill will or doubtful honesty.

Putting it all together, and with many examples, Hume declares that

It must . . . be allowed that every quality of the mind, which is *useful* or *agreeable* to the *person himself* or to *others*, communicates a pleasure to the spectator, engages his esteem, and is admitted under the honourable denomination of virtue or merit. (*EM* 9.12, p. 151)

Hume thinks that ethics is in this way a matter of which traits we admire and esteem, and which we hate. It is a matter of passion, not reason. His argument for this is that while the deliverances of experience and reason require *supplementing* by a passion to affect practice, morality is in itself practical, or in his sense, passionate. There is a difference between, for instance, on the one hand finding that the hotel bedroom is pink, and then liking or disliking it according to taste, and on the other hand finding that an action is forbidden or out of the question or beyond discussion, as this *already* settles the direction of the pressure on action: these are the words of people who already have a passion – they are set against the action. Ethical verdicts, including the names of the vices and virtues, include a 'valency' or direction: like love and hate, they point us towards or away from things. The function of ethics is to adjust our passions, to make us feel our common humanity, to respond to the villainy of Iago or the nobility of Antigone by our 'fellow feeling' with the other people on whom they impinge, and then to have within ourselves, by a process of contagion, a like repulsion from behaving in the worse ways, and a desire to imitate the better.

Some philosophers have overdone the influence of the moral emotions. They have found it impossibly difficult to understand 'weakness of will' or our capacity to succumb to temptation, knowingly doing what we believe to be wrong. As usual, Hume gets it right. He has no problem admitting our human weaknesses: on the contrary, the thing that needs more explaining is our strength, our ability to do our duty, to meet our obligations, even when these lie across our direct interest and thwart our strong desires. When we knowingly succumb to temptation, we lose a little tussle with part of ourselves, just as when we throw prudence to the winds and knowingly lay up trouble for ourselves in the future. As we all know, 'It is seldom men heartily love what lies at a distance from them, and what no way redounds to their particular benefit' (*T* III.iii.1, p. 583). It is no surprise that we often cannot summon up the energy to push forward our own concerns, let alone those of others. As I like to put it, when we knowingly succumb to temptation, just as when we deliberately hurt someone we love, things are out of joint. But a joint can only be out because normally it is not. We might hurt those we love, but unless we mostly do not and mostly feel uncomfortable when we do, the diagnosis of love starts to fade. It is the same with trespassing against our own better natures. Do it too often or too easily, and you extinguish the idea that you have a better nature at all.

I mentioned how Hume's revolutionary assessment of reason and passion broke with both his predecessors. His approach to moral philosophy marks a similarly decisive break from classical and medieval thought. Both in the classical thinkers and in the Christian tradition, it was hard to know virtue. Indeed, it was the preserve of the elite, those of special wisdom and rational gifts in the Greeks, or those given a special grace according to the Christians. Hume is more democratic. It is not difficult at all to determine which qualities of mind are useful or agreeable to ourselves or others. We know in general terms when life goes well or badly. And we therefore know as well which traits of mind help, and which stand in the way. The foundation stones of moral knowledge lie in front of everyone.

7

CONVENTION AND OBLIGATION

I observe, that it will be for my interest to leave another in the possession of his goods, *provided* he will act in the same manner with
regard to me. He is sensible of a like interest in the regulation of his
conduct. When this common sense of interest is mutually expressed,
and is known to both, it produces a suitable resolution and behaviour. And this may properly enough be called a convention or
agreement betwixt us, tho' without the interposition of a promise;
since the actions of each of us have a reference to those of the other,
and are performed upon the supposition, that something is to be
performed on the other part. Two men, who pull the oars of a boat,
do it by an agreement or convention, tho' they have never given
promises to each other. Nor is the rule concerning the stability of
possession the less derived from human conventions, that it arises
gradually, and acquires force by a slow progression, and by our
repeated experience of the inconveniences of transgressing it. On
the contrary, this experience assures us still more, that the sense of
interest has become common to all our fellows, and gives us a confidence of the future regularity of their conduct: And it is only on the
expectation of this, that our moderation and abstinence are founded.
In like manner are languages gradually established by human conventions without any promise. In like manner do gold and silver
become the common measures of exchange, and are esteemed sufficient payment for what is of a hundred times their value.

T III.ii.2, p. 490

We saw in the previous chapter that Hume's entry point in ethics is not through notions like duty and obligation, but through the way we feel about different traits of character. It is the love or aversion that they inspire that determine what we feel proud or ashamed of doing, and that thereby put pressure on our practical lives.

Sometimes the transition from talking of a virtue to talking of an obligation or duty is fairly straightforward. It is a good trait to feel gratitude towards a benefactor, and a bad trait not to show it, through indolence or inattention. So we can say that the recipient of the benefit *ought* to be grateful, and *ought* to do something to show his gratitude, or equally that he is under an obligation or has a duty to reciprocate in this way. It may seem strange to talk of being under an obligation to *feel* a certain way, but people who do not will attract criticism and sanctions, or anger and resentment, which are the primary symptoms of someone under an obligation. And after all, even the Bible talks of the duty of loving our neighbour. Replying that we're sorry but we can't bring ourselves to feel grateful, or care about our neighbour, is not much of an excuse. Others will look on us askance.

But one of Hume's most original contributions to social and political theory, as well as to moral philosophy, does not lie in the sphere of natural virtues such as gratitude, but in the sphere of what he called 'artificial virtues'. These are virtues associated with conformity to institutions and arrangements, or conventions, that have become established amongst people. The three that especially concerned him were the institution of promising, that of property, and the notion of allegiance to government, including the obligation to obey the law.

Hume wants a good account of the way they arise and the way they function. They have this peculiarity, that it takes some kind of reference to the behaviour of others for actions in accordance with them to have any utility. More precisely, it will be advantageous to me to perform a part *provided* that you perform likewise. Otherwise I simply lose out. Hume uses the analogy with an arch in which each stone plays a supportive role, *provided* other stones do likewise (*EM*, Appendix 3, p. 171). If they fail, then its supporting function fails with them. Once we think about it, it is plain that many of our actions, including ones that are simply second nature to us, have this conditional nature. If we coordinate our hunting, it is useful for me to stand where we planned, but only provided you do so as well. If you promise to do something for me, it is sensible of me to expect you to do it, provided your word means something to you. If I suppose it was simply a strategy to get me to put down my arms or lay myself open to some other plot, then it will not. If I work for you in return for a piece of coin or paper money, it only makes sense if other persons will in turn provide goods and services for me in return for the same coin or piece of paper.

These conditional arrangements require a special 'genealogy' or evolutionary story explaining how they might get going. So imagine the original situation of a 'war of all against all'. Suppose a bleak conflict, with no history of cooperation and no culture binding me to you, and suppose my interests are contrary to yours: I want something for myself, and you want it for yourself. We keep fighting. It would be better if we could devise some mode of living together. So suppose I 'promise' to lay down my arms, not to pursue my interest any more. How could this be more than an invitation to you to triumph over me? Or at best, a potential trap to lure you into laying down your arms, enabling me to spring a surprise on you? Either way, it would be a charade, a fake appearance of promising. A very clear model of this is visible in the familiar 'prisoners' dilemma', where even if the prisoners are allowed to get together and 'promise' to stand firm and not to confess, each still has just the same motivation to do so. And even if the situation is not quite that of a prisoners' dilemma, so that each of us would prefer to relax into a situation of peaceful cooperation, we may still think we risk too much by pursuing it.[26]

The task for a theory of cooperation, as Hume saw, must be to sketch a natural mechanism in which cooperation can emerge without a miracle. Simply suggesting that 'reason' enables us to find a solution is useless: we cannot sit down and promise to keep promises. A cooperative equilibrium needs other mechanisms of the mind to sustain it.

In Hume's account, cooperation and forbearance, and eventually the conventions of abiding by promises and respecting established property rights, arise from individual self-interest allied with foresight. They do not arise from altruism: although Hume did think we have benevolent tendencies, he has no wish to rely upon them in his account of the institutions associated with justice. Nor do they arise inevitably. Hume talks of a slow growth, and in situations of competition and conflict there is always the temptation to snatch the quick advantage and run. It is only with repeated interactions that confidence can grow. We have to learn to become trustworthy incrementally, bit by bit, by education in the advantages it gives. When the situation is bleak enough, the opportunity for repetition, practice, imitation, and education is not available. It is indeed too risky to offer the first move towards peace, and we simply continue in the war of all against all.

Thus imagine a room with a set of tables, at each of which a number of persons are engaged in some version of a prisoners' dilemma game. In this structure, the social payoff (the total gathered by the table) is greatest if each cooperates with the others. But everyone can do better for themselves, on each play, by 'defecting' or cheating, breaking the implicit agreement. If we imagine plays repeated, then the social goods pile up on the first kind of table, while those at the tables with defectors stay impoverished. If we then imagine a dynamic whereby cooperators are invited to cooperating tables and defectors are banished to defecting tables, the room will tend to split into two kinds: all cooperating and all defecting. But if we then suppose an evolutionary dynamic – suppose people leave offspring in numbers proportional to their chips – gradually the room fills with cooperating tables. Nice guys finish first.

Hume was very proud of the mechanism he sketches, returning to it in almost the same words as those quoted (*EM*, Appendix 3, p. 172). And rightly so, since he was the pioneer, and modern stories about the evolution of cooperation tread in exactly the same footsteps.[27] Hume also grafted onto the mechanism the additional insight that once we have a habit of one of these kinds, such as reliance on promises of forbearance from goods used by others, the idea of obligation quickly follows on. We ourselves might shrink from being the first to break the pattern, and might shun and penalize others who do so. A social norm builds up, and this plays its own roles in our motivations, cementing the habit into place with external sanctions and internal pressures of shame and guilt. The result may not be watertight, and then we are faced with the bogey whom Hume calls the 'sensible knave':

> Treating vice with the greatest candour, and making it all possible concessions, we must acknowledge, that there is not, in any instance, the smallest pretext for giving it the preference above virtue, with a view to self-interest; except, perhaps, in the case of justice, where a man, taking things in a certain light, may often seem to be a loser by his integrity. And though it is allowed, that, without a regard to property, no society could subsist; yet, according to the imperfect way in which human affairs are conducted, a sensible knave, in particular incidents, may think that an act of iniquity or infidelity will make a considerable addition to his fortune, without causing any considerable breach in the social union and confederacy. That *honesty is the best policy*, may be a good general rule; but is liable to many exceptions: and he, it may perhaps be thought, conducts himself with most wisdom, who observes the general rule, and takes advantage of all the exceptions. (*EM* 9.22, p. 155)

Finding an argument to stop the sensible knave in his tracks is something of a Holy Grail for moral philosophy, and the ambition of many 'cognitivist' or 'rationalist' moralists, convinced that pure reason, some consideration derived a priori from the nature of human agency, will show that the knave is in some subtle sense acting inconsistently, doing something parallel to contradicting himself in the sphere of belief. Hume, by contrast, is gloriously relaxed about it, immediately replying:

> I must confess, that, if a man think, that this reasoning much requires an answer, it will be a little difficult to find any, which

will to him appear satisfactory and convincing. If his heart rebel
not against such pernicious maxims, if he feel no reluctance to
the thoughts of villany or baseness, he has indeed lost a consid-
erable motive to virtue; and we may expect, that his practice will
be answerable to his speculation. But in all ingenuous natures,
the antipathy to treachery and roguery is too strong to be counter-
balanced by any views of profit or pecuniary advantage. Inward
peace of mind, consciousness of integrity, a satisfactory review of
our own conduct; these are circumstances, very requisite to happiness, and will be cherished and cultivated by every honest man,
who feels the importance of them. (*EM* 9.23, p. 155)

In other words, if we have a sensible knave on our hands, it is too
late. For some reason this person's sentiments or passions have not
progressed beyond the selfish here and now. The normal processes
of establishing a common humanity have failed, and the usual
mechanisms of shame and the ability to sustain a satisfactory review
of his own conduct are too weak. There is nothing more to say, as
the Grail seekers all eventually find. On this matter, Hume is close
to Aristotle in prioritizing early education and practice in the paths
of virtue over late and probably futile attempts to argue the villain
back into them. What is wrong with the knave is not that he has
subtly trespassed against reason, but that he is a knave.

And so we get a story in which the obligations of justice evolve.
It is a story that only builds on known mechanisms of the mind –
self-interest allied with foresight. But by the end, promises, property, and justice take on a life of their own. They provide
motivations that can constrain us even against our own interest. It
would not do to transgress against them. Unlike Nietzsche's
debunking genealogy of Christian ethics, Hume's genealogy is a
vindication of where we have arrived: we should be proud of
having built the arch, inventing and then sustaining the institutions
that keep cooperative social life in place. Eventually those institutions involve not only contracts, or promises, and property, but
also government and the allegiance to government and law. This
likewise answers to a need: the need for a mechanism assuring

everyone that everyone else is doing their bit in common enter-
prises, such as defence or the preservation of public safety, and that
the institutions of property, including transfer and disposition of
property, have their necessary detail.

Hume's evolutionary story leaves him at odds with the 'social
contract' tradition in political philosophy, as it appeared the century before in Hobbes and Locke, and in his contemporary
Rousseau.[28] Hobbes thinks in terms of people designing their way
out of the war of all against all, and has people voluntarily putting
themselves in the power of an absolute sovereign. Locke requires
tacit assent to the prevailing social order, which is thought of as a
contract between the ruler and the ruled. Rousseau eventually
advocates a kind of submission of the citizen to the general will, an
ongoing process of totalitarianism that eventually validated the
excesses of the French revolution. Hume substitutes for all this
hyperbole the calm fact that when government works to sustain
social life, its evident utility is all that is needed to justify it, and all
that does so. And it has to go catastrophically wrong before revolution is a better alternative.

Hume cherished the structures that sustain our social life. He was
in this respect deeply conservative, in the good sense of conserva-
tionist of the shapes and forms which these institutions have taken.
And of course he was deeply mistrustful of any scatterbrained project of doing better, for instance by promoting anarchism or society
without government or law, or dismantling the institutions of contract or private property. He would have had absolutely no patience
with the contemporary takeover of social ideals by monetary and
market values. When free-marketeers say that there is no such
thing as society, they are denying the very arches needed to
sustain contracts, law, government, and markets in the first place,
and then knavery loses its stigma, and we may well expect the worst,
as their practice becomes 'answerable to their speculation'.

8

OF MIRACLES

The plain consequence is (and it is a general maxim worthy of our attention), 'That no testimony is sufficient to establish a miracle, unless the testimony be of such a kind, that its falsehood would be more miraculous, than the fact, which it endeavours to establish: And even in that case, there is a mutual destruction of arguments, and the superior only gives us an assurance suitable to that degree of force, which remains, after deducting the inferior.' When anyone tells me, that he saw a dead man restored to life, I immediately consider with myself, whether it be more probable, that this person should either deceive or be deceived, or that the fact, which he relates, should really have happened. I weigh the one miracle against the other; and according to the superiority, which I discover, I pronounce my decision, and always reject the greater miracle. If the falsehood of his testimony would be more miraculous, than the event which he relates; then, and not till then, can he pretend to command my belief or opinion.

E 10, p. 173

Hume's sceptical discussion of miracles comes as section 10 of the *Enquiry Concerning Human Understanding*. It is now a classic, but in its own time it was regarded as particularly scandalous, and as Hume recounted in his short autobiography, 'answers by Reverends and Right Reverends came out two or three in a Year'.[29] We shall find that the Reverends and Right Reverends were well advised to worry.

Hume had by his own account discovered the central argument of the essay about a dozen years before, while he was composing the *Treatise*, but he suppressed it in the earlier work. His account of its discovery is worth quoting in full:

> I was walking in the cloister of the Jesuits' College of La Flèche, a town in which I passed two years of my youth, and engaged in conversation with a Jesuit of some parts and learning, who was relating to me, and urging some nonsensical miracle performed in their convent, when I was tempted to dispute against him; and as my head was full of the topics of my *Treatise of Human Nature*, which I was at that time composing, this argument immediately occurred to me, and I thought it very much gravelled my companion; but at last he observed to me, that it was impossible for the argument to have any solidity, because it operated equally against the Gospel as the Catholic Miracles; – which observation I thought proper to admit as a sufficient answer.[30]

Hume thought of the Christian religion, and others, as having two pillars to stand upon. One is 'revelation', and the other is a cluster of arguments from the nature of things up to the existence of a Supreme Being or beings, going under the heading of 'natural religion', or in other words religion as vindicated by the light of reason. The argument about miracles is designed to knock away the first of these. The other, 'natural religion', is immediately dealt with in 'Of Particular Providence and a Future State', which is the following section of the *Enquiry*, and eventually at greater length in the *Dialogues*.

Revelation, in religious contexts, can come in two forms, either directly, in some kind of personal illumination, or indirectly, through the oral or written tradition or the testimony of others, and it is this testimony that Hume's argument considers. His particular subject is the way in which the authentic nature of some revelation is supposed to be certified by the occurrence of suitable supernatural events. The prophet, saviour, or saint, God's conduit to earth, establishes his (or, less commonly, her) credentials by working miracles: raising the dead, walking on water, turning one substance into another, parting

IT IS ONE "MIRACLE" TO RAISE LAZARUS FROM THE DEAD, BUT IT IS A "HIGHER" FORM OF MIRACLE TO RAISE YOURSELF FROM THE DEAD

the sea, cursing things that then wither and die, flying through the air, covering huge distances in the blink of an eye, prophesying, and so on and so on. To be appropriate signs of special divine intervention in the world, these events have to be quite out of the ordinary run of things. They have to be contrary to the way of the world as we normally find it. They need to be astonishing.

A short response would be to say that these events are out and out impossible, and there is an end of it. Misreadings of Hume as saying just this have arisen because he sometimes expresses himself in similarly strong terms. For example, towards the end of the chapter he talks of some miracles surrounding the tomb of the Abbé de Paris, which had made a great stir in France at the time he first arrived there, and asks rhetorically, 'And what have we to oppose to such a cloud of witnesses, but the absolute impossibility or miraculous nature of the events, which they relate?' (*E* 10, p. 180). But this passage occurs *after* the argument is over. It is no more than a perfectly natural expression of natural belief: it is what any of us might say if, for instance, an acquaintance turned up telling us that the previous evening he lost a leg but it fortunately grew back.

Naturally Hume is in no position to insist a priori that *any* consistently described event is impossible. If there is no contradiction in the supposition that an event occurred, then for all reason can tell us in advance, it might occur. According to him, the question of whether events of any particular kind actually do occur is always one for experience to settle. Hence the issue has to be fought not on the question of whether miracles are possible, but whether we can be assured that they have happened.

A slightly longer sceptical response to the teller of miracles, then, would be to say that experience has given the laws of nature such backing that nothing whatsoever should shake our faith in them. They would have become certain, accorded a status beyond the reach of contrary evidence. Here too there is scope for misreadings, and misinterpretations of the work have resulted from them. They arise because earlier in the work, Hume distinguishes proof and probability, saying that we can talk of proof whenever we have such 'arguments from experience as leave no room for doubt or

opposition'. He cites fire burning, water suffocating, and the production of motion by impulse and gravity as reasonable candidates
(*E* 6, p. 132). Does this mean that we have our proof that any
alleged miracle did not happen, so that's the end of it? Not at all. In
the context of reports of miracles, there evidently *has* arisen doubt
and opposition – that's exactly what the reporter is expressing.
There is a report of the saint not being consumed by fire, or of
water not suffocating, or whatever it may be. Here Hume says, if
the testimony is strong enough to have the same status, it would be
a question of 'proof against proof, of which the strongest must pre-
vail, but still with a diminution of its force, in proportion to that of
its antagonist' (*E* 10, p. 173). In other words, nothing is beyond discussion or ruled out in advance. We are to be in the business of
balancing the testimony against the experience of uniformity.
'Proof' may *normally* leave no room for doubt, but in the context
of assessing what to believe when doubt and opposition does arise,
it works simply as a very high probability, and can be opposed or
diminished by evidence as all probabilities can.

Hume gives an excellent example of a view that would have been
thought sufficiently proved by experience at a particular place and
time, namely that water does not suddenly turn solid. An 'Indian
prince' would have been absolutely within his rights to believe that
with as much conviction as any other empirical law, having never
been anywhere approaching freezing point. But further experience,
such as a trip to Moscow in winter, would obviously raise doubt and
opposition, and eventually show that under these new circumstances,
water does suddenly turn solid. But if the Indian prince could not
travel to see it for himself, but had to rely on testimony, then the testimony would need to be pretty convincing to overcome the
hitherto uniform evidence of his senses that nothing of the kind
happens. Hume does not believe that there is any kind of safe haven
for any empirical truths, as if they have an electric fence around
them that no evidence can penetrate. Right from the very beginning
of his chapter it is a question of balancing of one piece of evidence
against another.[31]

For Hume, the occurrence of a piece of testimony is one event.

Whatever it testifies for would be another, which may or may not have happened. The testimony tends to raise the probability that it did happen, for in general people are pretty reliable. That is why we can have confidence in general in the reports of others, and why it is very difficult for us, traumatic even, to think that our informants are deceiving us, or are themselves deceived. But, and here is the rub, we know that this is the kind of thing that happens. We do not preserve a childhood faith in the uniform accuracy and sincerity of other people's reports. The business of law courts and historians would be over much more quickly if we did. But as we all know, people lie. Mistakes occur. Eyewitnesses misreport what they saw. Indeed, eyewitness reports often vary with information and misinformation introduced after the event. Witnesses disagree. Reports get garbled in transmission. Memory confabulates. Facts are suppressed. Fictions are taken for histories. The more psychologists have investigated our functioning in these respects, the more pessimistic they have become about our natural reliability. In other words, just as a court of law may need to balance a testimony on one side against a similar testimony, or other sources of probability, on the other side, so does the historian trying to assess the credibility of the testimony to an event, and especially any marvellous or near miraculous event.

The essence of Hume's thought is that since a miraculous event is clean contrary to the normal run of things, the testimony needs to be correspondingly strong on the other side. It needs to have a weight which really puts it into contention against the weight of the opposing experience. A court of law may usually accept my testimony that I was somewhere on such and such a day. But if I say I was on Mars, then there is a problem. The near impossibility of what I am claiming quite outweighs any sign of sincerity that I manage. This is the common-sense approach to outlandish stories that Hume distils into the principle quoted at the head of the chapter, identifying the hurdle that testimony to a miracle needs to overcome. It needs to be such that the falsity of the testimony would be as extraordinary, as clean contrary to the run of things, as miraculous in fact, as the event to which it testifies.

This principle sets a high hurdle, clearly enough. But Hume does

not go on to say that testimony cannot overcome it (another preva-
lent misreading). In fact, he states just the opposite. He cites the
possibility of a mysterious eclipse:

> Thus, suppose, all authors, in all languages, agree, that, from the
> first of JANUARY 1600, there was a total darkness over the whole
> earth for eight days: Suppose that the tradition of this extraordinary
> event is still strong and lively among the people: That all travellers,
> who return from foreign countries, bring us accounts of the same
> tradition, without the least variation or contradiction: It is evident,
> that our present philosophers, instead of doubting the fact, ought to
> receive it as certain, and ought to search for the causes whence it
> might be derived. (*E* 10, p. 184)

Independence is very hard to establish, but it would have been evi-
denced in those days by the diverse geographical origins of the
reports. Given, then, that these reports are truly independent – there
could have been no collusion of witnesses, conscious or uncon-
scious – then the consilience between them requires explaining, and
it is hard to think of anything but the common sighting of the same
astronomical phenomenon that might explain it. But Hume admits
the exception precisely to point up the contrast with typical reports
of alleged supernatural miracles. Indeed, it is impossible not to think
that he had in mind the very pointed contrast with the marked
absence of such independent confirmation, for instance by Roman
historians, of the multitude of miracles surrounding the early years of
Christianity. As the supremely ironic Roman historian Gibbon, a
fervent disciple of Hume, notoriously put it, thereby getting himself
into a lot of hot water:

> The lame walked, the blind saw, the sick were healed, the dead
> were raised, demons were expelled, and the laws of Nature were
> frequently suspended for the benefit of the Church. But the sages
> of Greece and Rome turned aside from the awful spectacle, and
> pursuing the ordinary occupations of life and study, appeared
> unconscious of any alterations in the moral or physical government

of the world. Under the reign of Tiberius, the whole earth, or at least a celebrated province of the Roman empire, was involved in a preternatural darkness of three hours. Even this miraculous event, which ought to have excited the wonder, the curiosity and the devotion of mankind, passed without notice in an age of science and history.[32]

So in the second part of Hume's chapter, the question is not whether testimony *could in principle* overcome the hurdle set at the end of the first part, but whether the testimony for religious miracles ever actually *does* so. Hume lists the kind of thing that might help: a miracle attested to by sufficient number of men of such

unquestioned good sense, education, and learning, as to secure us against all delusion in themselves; of such undoubted integrity as to place them beyond all suspicion of any design to deceive others; of such credit and reputation in the eyes of mankind, as to have a great deal to lose in case of their being detected in any falsehood; and at the same time, attesting facts, performed in such a public manner, and in so celebrated a part of the world, as to render the detection unavoidable. (*E* 10, p. 174)

Putting on his hat as a historian, Hume thinks this has never happened.

So why is belief in miracles so widespread? Perhaps we are naturally credulous, programmed by nature to accept testimony without question, even in the most outrageous cases.[33] And there may be mistakes in our assessment of a situation. A common mistake is to take a story, in which it might be said that many people of credit witnessed some event, at face value, forgetting the role of the narrator of the story: one chronicler's story saying that a hundred people were present and each saw the miracle gives us one testimony, not a hundred independent testimonies. But Hume has a more interesting point to hand. He makes a groundbreaking early foray into what has now become the science of cognitive dysfunction, by highlighting the influence of the passions on our propensity to believe things.

Miraculous "stroke of luck" — I just came late for a plane flight that crashes. ← VS —
I arrive on time for a flight that finishes uneventfully. BORING / etc.

We, or the less careful among us, believe such things because our minds are swayed by the passions of surprise and wonder. These render reports of miracles especially agreeable. We, or the majority of mankind, actively *want* to be amazed. We like the extraordinary. It is *interesting*. Believing it is *fun*. In support of this piece of psychological observation, Hume cites the charming example of rumours without foundation, such as gossip of marriages spreading around country towns. The same influence of the passions helps to explain why stories of miracles take wing. It is such fun to tell them, just as for many people it is fun to recount amazing coincidences, horoscopes, dreams that came true, and the like. Of course, historically, telling of supernatural happenings has been not only fun, but has had other functions as well, such as marginalizing and eventually bringing about the persecution and murder of people on the grounds of their alleged demonic powers. Fear and hatred can mix with human fun.

There are other temptations as well: 'The wise lend a very academic faith to any report that flatters the passions of the reporter . . . But what greater temptation than to appear a missionary, a prophet, an ambassador from heaven?' (*E* 10, p. 182). It is more than just fun to present yourself as having a hotline to the Supreme Being. As the example of revivalist preachers shows, it brings self-importance, adulation, power, followers, sexual conquests, and wealth.

Hume's account of our cognitive shortfalls is helped by his account of belief itself in functional terms. That makes it easy for him to see the influence of passion on belief: he is not hindered by a rigid split between exercises of reason on the one hand, responsible for belief, and then away in a quite different part of our brains or our systems, our passions entirely insulated from all that. For Hume there is no bar against a desire that something be true influencing the 'strength and vivacity' with which our imagining that it is true is invested – eventually turning a mere idea into a fully fledged belief. It is just a question of experience whether this happens, and that indeed confirms that it does. We need only think of the way people eagerly lap up confirming evidence, and dismiss countervailing evidence, for the variety of

Blair & Bush apparently convinced that
∫ Hussein had WMDs & intended to use them soon against the US & UK.

things they want to believe. Beloved national leaders come to mind, but are not atypical.

a .
002/3

Hume cites other problems for anyone relying on such testimony. One is that the miracles of each religion in a sense oppose those of the others. Protestants of his time rubbished specifically Catholic miracles. Each would have to rubbish pagan miracles, although according to Hume the testimony that the Emperor Vespasian had miraculous powers is at least as impressive as the testimony for any other miracle (*E* 10, p. 178). Nobody could be more zealous in detecting folly and fraud in others than someone concerned to protect his own monopoly of divinely aided powers.

It is hard to fault the reasoning in this extraordinary chapter, although of course many have tried from its first appearance to the present day. One puzzle is interesting enough to deserve some analysis. This is the problem advanced against Hume by Richard Price, a mathematician who first presented Thomas Bayes's fundamental work on the mathematics of probability to the Royal Society in 1763. Indeed Price, and possibly Bayes himself, the founder of one of the most important parts of probability theory, was clearly motivated by the wish to find an answer to Hume on the problem of induction and on the issue of miracles.[34] Price points out that we seem to have a counter to Hume in the fact that we often allow quite unremarkable, fallible testimony to certify even very improbable events. For example, a newspaper report of the number that won the lottery will be good enough for people to believe it, even if they hold their breath until confirmation comes in. Yet the newspaper may be only so-so reliable, and the antecedent probability of the number winning may be one in a million or ten million, or whatever was the number of tickets.

The full analysis of this is quite tricky, but the basic difference is easy to spot. The newspaper is going to report some number, and some number will have won. So if the newspaper is reasonably likely to get it right – let us say, four-fifths of the time – we have to compare the probability of its saying this number won and its having done so against the probability of its saying this number won and its not having done so. Now it is true that the antecedent probability of the number having won is very low. But then so is the antecedent probability of the newspaper saying it won – just as low, in fact. The number may be one of the ten million that could have won, but it is equally one of the ten million the newspaper might have reported as winning (a perfectly good second lottery could be run on the number that will be reported in the paper, and the odds against winning would be just the same as in the original lottery). When these are put in the equation, they cancel out, leaving the likelihood that the newspaper got it right just where it started, at four-fifths.

The difference is that in the miracle case there is no *datum* that anything antecedently improbable has happened. There is only the antecedent improbability of the occurrence of the story, which is not all that great, and certainly not comparable to the improbability of a good solid miracle, because we all know such stories are common. In the lottery case there is such an additional datum.

Bayes's analysis did make it plain that if in advance we thought 'miracles' are quite likely, then against that background much weaker testimony might reasonably impress us as good enough. If antecedently you expect Cambridge to be beset by flying pigs, then if I come in and tell you I was hit by one on the way to my lecture, you may be more inclined to believe me than if you had no antecedent intelligence of this plague. The question then would shift to the reliability of the antecedent belief. If you held this unhappy view of Cambridge because other people had told you they had seen such animals, then it is this piece of gullibility about which we should be sceptical, and your using it to confirm my accident just shows you acting true to form. Hume's culture (and ours, and many others') was one in which miracles were used as evidence for hot links to the supernatural, not one in which there were *other* reasons for identifying particular historical actors as having the supernatural on their side.

Readers new to the essay on miracles sometimes ask what relevance it would have if I, the subject, witnessed a miracle myself, or if I, the subject, felt within myself the power of revelation, the voice of God speaking. The blunt answer in the first case is that you are not going to do so. If you think you do, then you should treat the testimony of your senses in just the way he asks you to treat the testimony of others. Sometimes we shouldn't believe our eyes. I once enjoyed the privilege of sitting in the front row of a performance given by Ricky Jay, perhaps the greatest prestidigitator (manipulator and conjurer) of the day. I saw with my own eyes eggs appear out of thin air, shuffled packs of cards arrange themselves into suits, and so on. Or at least, that is what my eyes were telling me I saw. But I had no inclination to believe them. I had no idea what instead I was seeing, such was the performer's genius, but I wasn't in the least inclined to doubt that it was something other than the miracles on show. As for internal revelation, it is worth remembering that firstly, it is seldom free from the influence of testimony (Christians in rapture see and hear the kinds of thing put into the repertoire by their tradition; Muslims see something different, and so on across the world). An individual subject may be quite unable to resist the 'force and vivacity' of a moment of ecstatic revelation. But this does not exempt his resulting convictions from the cold light of likelihood, however hard it then is for him to shine that light himself.

Hume sums it all up with his superb irony:

> So that, upon the whole, we may conclude, that the CHRISTIAN religion not only was at first attended with miracles, but even at this day cannot be believed by any reasonable person without one. Mere reason is insufficient to convince us of its veracity: And whoever is moved by *Faith* to assent to it, is conscious of a continued miracle in his own person, which subverts all the principles of his understanding, and gives him a determination to believe what is most contrary to custom and experience. (*E* 10, p. 186)

But it is not a continued miracle, of course. It is just the sad but common fact that the kinds of cognitive dysfunction he has described distract our minds away from their usual, natural job of staying in harmony with the uniformities that nature displays. When people want to believe something, then eventually they will, and the armies of astrologers, clairvoyants, homeopaths, management consultants, holy men, and faith healers are ready for them.

9

NATURAL RELIGION

In a word, *Cleanthes*, a man, who follows your hypothesis, is able, perhaps, to assert, or conjecture, that the universe, sometime, arose from something like design: But beyond that position he cannot ascertain one single circumstance, and is left afterwards to fix every point of his theology, by the utmost license of fancy and hypothesis. This world, for aught he knows, is very faulty and imperfect, compared to a superior standard; and was only the first rude essay of some infant deity, who afterwards abandoned it, ashamed of his lame performance: It is the work only of some dependent, inferior deity; and is the object of derision to his superiors: It is the production of old age and dotage in some superannuated deity; and ever since his death, has run on at adventures, from the first impulse and active force which it received from him . . . You justly give signs of horror, *Demea*, at these strange suppositions; But these, and a thousand more of the same kind, are *Cleanthes*' suppositions, not mine. From the moment the attributes of the deity are supposed finite, all these have place. And I cannot, for my part, think that so wild and unsettled a system of theology is, in any respect, preferable to none at all.

D 5.22

Hume himself said that nothing could be more artful than his *Dialogues Concerning Natural Religion*, the incendiary work on arguments for the existence of a deity that he only allowed to be published after his death. It has proved sufficiently artful to prompt a whole variety of readings, from ones seeing Hume as an out and out atheist, to ones seeing him as a rather pallid kind of believer. I hold that when we take in the full measure of his argument, the correct reading stands out quite clearly. I also believe that the correct view brings to the forefront two of Hume's extraordinary qualities: his remarkable ability to transform a problem, and his beautiful economy of aim. For he both reconfigures standard debates about religion, in a way that is still not appreciated, and gives us what is needed, and no more, to justify his own scepticism about it.

The work consists of a series of conversations between three participants: Philo, a religious sceptic, Cleanthes, who defends the 'argument to design' for the existence of a deity, and Demea, who defends the idea that there is something like a mathematical or logical proof of the existence of the deity. Demea's position is much less important to Hume than the other pair, and this corresponds to the prevailing theological temper of his times. The showpiece of eighteenth-century theology was the argument to design: the view that the order of nature declared the Creator's glory. The harmonious motions of the stars and planets and the indefinitely complex and adapted complexities of animal life alike testify to the infinite power and wisdom of the divine architect. For just as the appearance of a ship or a timepiece gives us infallible reason to believe in design and workmanship, so the parallel organization of nature gives us infallible reason to believe in divine authorship. This argument is of course still rampant: it is the centrepiece of almost all contemporary evangelizing, and is the special exhibit of Creationists and so-called Intelligent Design cheerleaders.

For the greater part of the work – until the last of the twelve dialogues – Philo directs a withering battery of doubts at the argument to design. He points out that it is an argument by analogy, but that any analogy between a human construction and the whole frame of nature is stretched and tenuous. He points out that we cannot infer the unity of a designer from the fact of design: ships and watches are the product of countless designers offering generations of designs, gradually refining their predecessors in a process of trial and error. He asks about the lurking infinite regress of designers responsible for designers. He points out that insofar as the world 'resembles' any human construction, it resembles an animal or vegetable just as closely. He points out that design as we are familiar with it means human contrivance, which is just one rather limited, minuscule way in which things in one corner of the cosmos happen — so why make it the supreme model for the whole? He reminds us that in the world as we find it, minds depend upon bodies, not the other way around. He points out that the problem of reconciling the harsh ways of nature with an infinitely good, knowing, and capable deity is actually made much worse by reliance on the argument to design, since it is obviously impossible to infer God's boundless goodness from his often miserable and suffering creation. Yet this is what anyone relying on the design argument must do. He mocks the religious believer's attribution of human emotions such as jealousy and anger to the deity. For our sentiments 'are calculated for preserving the existence and promoting the activity' of ourselves in our situations. Since the monotheist's deity doesn't inhabit any particular natural or social niche, Demea drily points out that 'it seems unreasonable to transfer such sentiments to a supreme existence or to suppose him actuated by them' (D 3.13). All this is plain enough, and laid out with magisterial ease, and great comic effect, in the bulk of the text.

The difficulty of interpretation arises because after Philo has effectively destroyed the design argument, he simply turns around and admits its cogency. Furthermore, the debates are presented as witnessed by a young pupil, Pamphilius, who ends the work by judging that Cleanthes is nearest to the truth, apparently swimming completely against the actual current of the argument. So just when complete religious scepticism seems to triumph, Hume stays his hand, and even seems to allow his opponent to have the truth of the matter. It is most disconcerting. Indeed, it is tempting

*Christians, of course, attribute poor design + unhappiness to sin and The FALL of Adam + Eve — another flawed design.

to see Hume as deploying the distinction between philosophical reasoning and natural belief, which we met in chapter 4, in connection with the external world. Perhaps Philo is not so much sceptical about religious belief as he is about the power of reason to underwrite it, just as we have seen that Hume is sceptical not about the natural world, but about the power of reason to give a satisfactory theory of it. This would be a Hume who 'destroyed reason to make room for faith', and since the faith in question would be in no worse standing than faith in chairs and tables, so much the better.

The problem here could have been raised at the end of the last chapter. After all, we might have asked, what business has Hume to condemn exercises of superstition, or improbable beliefs formed under the influence of particular passions or ambitions? It is not as if he has a background of rational, probable beliefs against which to contrast these. On the contrary, if superstition and the mechanisms responsible for it are natural and pretty universal, why don't they gain the same status as beliefs in chairs and tables, or in the sun rising tomorrow? If we lose any sense of what we 'ought' to believe, how can we retain a sense of what we ought not to believe?

The difference is that people the world over submit to the same regime of natural belief: we all think of ourselves as inhabiting a space of relatively stable objects amongst which we move, and we all rely on everyday uniformities to continue in their familiar paths. But people do not all find the same supernatural world. Some find spirits, ghosts, and witches; others find one God, but one who carelessly tells different people different things, and others again find many gods. Once the detail comes in, no religion gets the protection of *universal*, *natural*, and *pragmatically essential* natural belief. Hence Hume's relentless and unmistakable contempt for religion and the religious spirit, at least as these are found in recorded history. Whereas natural belief is necessary for life, religious belief is far from it, and often the reverse. It gets in the way of humanity and benevolence, and opposes any natural dispositions of the mind, both as far as beliefs go and as far as sentiments and morals go. Religious belief simply does not get the protection from nature and from pragmatism that shelters natural belief in an external world.

So why does Philo seem to throw in the towel? Some interpret Hume as being simply cautious, covering his real scepticism with a transparently thin veneer of deference to religious belief. Had Hume published the work in his own lifetime, one could perhaps accept this. An ironic appearance of deference to conventional piety was certainly within Hume's repertoire, and was indeed quite a standard move amongst sceptical authors in the eighteenth century. But since he suppressed the work in any event, such a precaution would have been unnecessary.

The extraordinary reversal comes in the final dialogue. This is the sceptical Philo speaking:

> all the sciences almost lead us insensibly to acknowledge a first intelligent author; and their authority is often so much the greater, as they do not directly profess that intention . . . [T]o what pitch of pertinacious obstinacy must a philosopher in this age have attained, who can now doubt of a supreme intelligence? (D 12.2–3)

Hume well understood, and at least in that sense *sympathized* with, the appeal of the argument to design, although as a sceptic he must have been perfectly cheerful about the possibility that it leads us into an illusion. Are we to read this as indicating a residual religious spirit flickering in the depths of the great infidel? We must read on to Philo's next words:

> I ask the theist, if he does not allow, that there is a great and immeasurable, because incomprehensible difference between the *human* and the *divine* mind: The more pious he is, the more readily will he assent to the affirmative, and the more will he be disposed to magnify the difference: He will even assert, that the difference is of a nature, which cannot be too much magnified. I next turn to the atheist, who, I assert, is only nominally so, and

can never possibly be in earnest; and I ask him, whether from the coherence and apparent sympathy in all the parts of this world, there be not a certain degree of analogy among all the operations of nature, in every situation and in every age; whether the rotting of a turnip, the generation of an animal, and the structure of human thought, be not energies that probably bear some remote analogy to each other: It is impossible he can deny it: He will readily acknowledge it. Having obtained this concession, I push him still further in his retreat; and I ask him, if it be not probable, that the principle which first arranged, and still maintains order in this universe, bears not also some remote inconceivable analogy to the other operations of nature, and among the rest, to the economy of human mind and thought. However reluctant, he must give his assent. Where then, cry I to both these antagonists, is the subject of your dispute? The theist allows, that the original intelligence is very different from human reason: The atheist allows, that the original principle of order bears some remote analogy to it. Will you quarrel, Gentlemen, about the degrees, and enter into a controversy, which admits not of any precise meaning, nor consequently of any determination? (*D* 12.7)

At this point Hume is revealing the true point of application of his scepticism. This is *not* primarily about 'the existence of God'. The surprise is that this is no longer worth contending. It is about the implications – for practice, emotion, morals, hopes, fears, for the whole business of living – that are usually supposed to follow on from that. In other words, for the purpose of scepticism about the practices of 'vulgar' religion, Hume realizes *he does not need to contest* the bare assertion of the existence of God. That can be left lying on one side. It becomes a pointless issue so long as the argument to design gets you to no *usable* conception of the nature of a deity. As Wittgenstein said in a different context, nothing will do as well as something about which nothing can be said.

This is Hume's transformation of the subject. Natural religion relies on the powers of human reason to deliver belief in the existence and nature of God. It is this that concerns the *Dialogues*.

Hume destroys its importance, and so by the end does not even bother to fight about its truth – and that's the point of Philo's concessions. If Pamphilius awards the prize to Cleanthes, it is a supreme irony, because the judicious reader can see that by then all Cleanthes's teeth have been drawn: *he has become effectively indistinguishable from the sceptic Philo.*

This is of course a very surprising turn – so surprising that very few people who have argued about the existence of God have understood it, then or subsequently. They suppose that with the words 'God exists' come a whole crowd of implications: consolations for life's sufferings, things to expect, things to hope for, instructions how to behave, rituals to go in for, specially qualified experts in beards and skirts and sandals to tell you how to keep on the right side of the Supreme Being, and so on. But if the words signify no more than the conclusion of the design argument, nothing whatsoever follows. The most you have is something bearing a remote analogy to human intelligence, and to many other natural things such as planets or turnips, and which caused a world. If we can determine what to expect, how to behave, who to admire, which behaviour to reject, from the world as we experience it, well and good, and Hume as we have seen thought we could. But if you could not do so, then turning your gaze on the supernatural would not help. Either way, we are on our own.

Perhaps the clearest expression of this line of thought comes from section 11 ('Of a Particular Providence and of a Future State') of the *Enquiry Concerning Human Understanding*:

You find certain phænomena in nature. You seek a cause or author. You imagine that you have found him. You afterwards become so enamoured of this offspring of your brain, that you imagine it impossible, but he must produce something greater and more perfect than the present scene of things, which is so full of ill and disorder. You forget, that this superlative intelligence and benevolence are entirely imaginary, or, at least, without any foundation in reason; and that you have no ground to ascribe to him any qualities, but what you see he has actually exerted and

displayed in his productions. Let your gods, therefore, O philosophers, be suited to the present appearances of nature: And
presume not to alter these appearances by arbitrary suppositions,
in order to suit them to the attributes, which you so fondly ascribe
to your deities. (*E* 11, p. 191)

Hume gives the conclusion:

While we argue from the course of nature, and infer a particular
intelligent cause, which first bestowed, and still preserves order
in the universe, we embrace a principle, which is both uncertain
and useless. It is uncertain; because the subject lies entirely
beyond the reach of human experience. It is useless; because our
knowledge of this cause being derived entirely from the course of
nature, we can never, according to the rules of just reasoning,
return back from the cause with any new inference, or making
additions to the common and experienced course of nature,
establish any new principles of conduct and behaviour. (*E* 11,
p. 194)

Hume's transformation of the problem is the discovery that
humanity can only check out of Hotel Supernatural with
whichever baggage it brings with it. If you or your culture hate
homosexuals, that is what you will find when you interrogate
God's word, either as it bubbles up in your own brain, or as you
read the sacred texts. If you or your culture think women are of
less value than men, that is what you will find in turn. If you are
fed up with war, you will find instructions to turn the other
cheek; if later you are minded to steal your neighbours' land, then
turn the page and you will read God's word telling you to go right
ahead. If you are a slave-owning culture, you will find advice on
who to sell or where to buy slaves. If alongside your piety you
believe that witches blight crops, you will find a God who tells you
to kill witches.

Here as well we see the economy of Hume's aim. A lesser
thinker would do as most people do, which is to go bull-headed

Dawkins + Co.

at the issue of the existence of a deity, and parade more or less unconvincing proofs and disproofs. Scientists who fancy themselves as philosophers usually end up doing just that. Hume can dissect the arguments better than anyone. But he knows the results will be forever contested, and of course he is completely sceptical about anyone's ability to prove a positive or negative result in these cloudy regions. So what he does instead is to show that the outcome simply does not matter. He discards what he does not need. He can afford to, for he has enough cards left to win the trick. What matters are the alleged implications people wish to draw from their deity. But by directing his scepticism at those implications, Hume simply eviscerates the issue.

Since the point is surprising, it is worth approaching from a different angle. A religion may tell us that something exists. But the important bit is what we are then supposed to do about it. This is always in the hands of interpreters, usually elderly men in skirts and sandals. They specify rituals to be performed, sacrifices to make, conduct to observe, symbols to adore, things to fear, people to persecute, sayings to repeat. They tell of ways to salvation, or damnation. This is the bit that matters: people can get killed for doubting it or disagreeing with it or mocking it. But the point is that by now the whole practice has floated free of any actual *entity*. A myth does as well as anything real, sustaining the practice, validating the bearded men with the skirts and sandals. So we misdirect our batteries if we bother about the 'ontological' question of God's existence. It is only what people make of it that counts; and for them to make whatever they do of it, a real deity and a virtual deity are equally good. It is the practice which makes life go better or worse. The ontology no longer matters to the bit that does matter.

Key

So Hume is not a 'dogmatic' atheist, and still less some fellow-travelling theist. Neither position fits him as a sceptic. The position that does fit is that of denying that *anything* the theist supposes to follow from his bare, and barely intelligible, claim of existence, really does so. What it comes down to is that the 'religious spirit' is to be regarded not as metaphysical speculation, but in terms of the ethics associated with it at particular times and places. By itself, the bare affirmation that God exists, and for that matter the bare denial of it, neither add nor subtract from such ethics. As with his theory of causation, it is what we do with religious belief that matters. Metaphysics is a useless addendum, and that includes the metaphysics of theological reality.

Humanity's gods are dangerous things. They magnify our moral demands, shouting them through a megaphone, as it were. So in the *Dialogues*, Cleanthes tries the moral tack of supposing that religion, with the promise of heaven or the threat of hell, eternal sticks and carrots, 'however corrupted', is better than no religion at all:

> For if finite and temporary rewards and punishments have so great an effect, as we daily find: How much greater must be expected from such as are infinite and eternal? (*D* 12.10)

Philo denies the psychology. Human beings are adapted to care about the here and now, not about anything both speculative and a long way away. He reinforces the point with a piece of common observation:

> Factions, civil wars, persecutions, subversions of government, oppression, slavery; these are the dismal consequences which always attend [religion's] prevalency over the minds of men. If the religious spirit be ever mentioned in any historical narration, we are sure to meet afterwards with a detail of the miseries, which attend it. And no period of time can be happier or more prosperous, than those in which it is never regarded, or heard of. (*D* 12.11)

And when Cleanthes says, rather unconvincingly, that this is just false religion, religion getting out of hand, Philo replies that it always does, and worse than that, religions impose their own ideas of piety and virtue:

> But even though superstition or enthusiasm should not put itself in direct opposition to morality; the very diverting of the attention,

the raising up a new and frivolous species of merit, the prepos-
terous distribution which it makes of praise and blame, must
have the most pernicious consequences, and weaken extremely
men's attachment to the natural motives of justice and humanity.

Such a principle of action likewise, not being any of the familiar motives of human conduct, acts only by intervals on the
temper, and must be roused by continual efforts, in order to
render the pious zealot satisfied with his own conduct, and make
him fulfil his devotional task. Many religious exercises are entered
into with seeming fervour, where the heart, at the time, feels cold
and languid: A habit of dissimulation is by degrees contracted;
And fraud and falsehood become the predominant principle.
Hence the reason of that vulgar observation, that the highest zeal
in religion and the deepest hypocrisy, so far from being inconsistent, are often or commonly united in the same individual
character. (*D* 12.16–17)

Superstition, in Hume, is associated with idolatry, and the
descendants of idolatry in the ceremonies and rituals of the
Roman Catholic Church. Hume is contemptuous enough of
those, but he loathed even more the spirit of 'enthusiasm': the
vainglorious conviction that direct conversation with the Lord and
therefore direct instructions on conduct belonged to the privileged
elect of the Presbyterian and Puritan congregations. With superstition comes blind obedience to the priest; with enthusiasm
comes licence and fantastic schemes of living without tradition or
ordinary morality. There is some evidence that while he was writing his history of the seventeenth century, Hume came to see
enthusiasm as such a pestilential disease in the body politic that he
actually softened his opposition to superstition, as the lesser of two
evils. There was certainly enough zealotry in the Scotland of his
times to prompt such a movement. It was less than ten years after
Hume died that Robert Burns definitively described the small-
minded, vindictive, hypocritical, lascivious Presbyterian church
elder in 'Holy Willie's Prayer'. And there is much more scattered
through Hume's works about the dismal effects of the religious

spirit, and the way in which religious duty typically excludes 'all the general precepts of charity and benevolence'. In fact, the utmost a 'wise magistrate' can do is to make a saving game of it, and keep the religious spirit as far as possible from the business of government.

If, as I have been arguing, the *Dialogues* simply amplify an attitude to religion and its defences that is present throughout Hume's published writings, why might he have allowed publication only after his death? For thirty years or so he had published other sceptical works on religion, including two chapters ('Of Miracles' and 'Of a Particular Providence and of a Future State') of his *Enquiry* which are calculated to jar on religious sensibilities just as badly as anything in the *Dialogues*. By the time of his last decade he was a Grand Old Man in Edinburgh and had very little to lose whether he published or not, whereas at the time of his *Enquiry* (1749) he had good reason to worry about his future career. Perhaps the answer is politeness, or friendship with ministers of the moderate wing of the Church of Scotland. Perhaps he was just tired of controversy. Or perhaps he feared, prophetically, that his message would not get through, and had no relish for the disappointment of seeing yet another of his philosophical works misunderstood and traduced. We know for sure that he foresaw that. In a famous letter to a mutual friend, Adam Smith describes how, when Hume was near death, he amused himself by imagining the excuses for delay that he might give to Charon, the mythical ferryman who took the souls of the dead to the underworld:

He then diverted himself with inventing several jocular excuses, which he supposed he might make to Charon, and with imagining the very surly answers which it might suit the character of Charon to return to them. 'Upon further consideration,' said he, 'I thought I might say to him, Good Charon, I have been correcting my works for a new edition. Allow me a little time, that I may see how the public receives the alterations.' But Charon would answer, 'When you have seen the effect of these, you will be for making other alterations. There will be no end of such excuses;

so, honest friend, please step into the boat.' But I might still urge, 'Have a little patience, good Charon; I have been endeavoring to open the eyes of the public. If I live a few years longer, I may have the satisfaction of seeing the downfall of some of the prevailing systems of superstition.' But Charon would then lose all temper and decency. 'You loitering rogue, that will not happen these many hundred years. Do you fancy I will grant you a lease for so long a term? Get into the boat this instant, you lazy loitering rogue.'[35]

Hume was right: within forty years of his death the revivalism of the nineteenth century ushered in the dismal years of Victorian religiosity, and Europe seemed to forget the lessons it could so easily have learned the century before.

Taken together, the discussion of miracles and that of 'natural religion' annihilate the attempt to found religion on reason. But Hume does much more. He also invites us to see the mechanisms of mind responsible for religions as far removed from those that adapt us to coping in the natural world, or for living on a decent footing with each other. They may at best be the unfortunate by-products of tendencies that stand us in reasonably good stead when confined to other subject matters. And we surely cannot deny that, whether they exist or not, our Gods reflect little credit on us.

CF: FRANK TUREK + CO.

10

TASTE

There is a species of philosophy, which cuts off all hopes of success in such an attempt, and represents the impossibility of ever attaining any standard of taste. The difference, it is said, is very wide between judgment and sentiment. All sentiment is right; because sentiment has a reference to nothing beyond itself, and is always real, wherever a man is conscious of it . . . [A] thousand different sentiments, excited by the same object, are all right: Because no sentiment represents what is really in the object. It only marks a certain conformity or relation between the object and the organs or faculties of the mind; and if that conformity did not really exist, the sentiment could never possibly have being. Beauty is no quality in things themselves: It exists merely in the mind which contemplates them; and each mind perceives a different beauty.

ST 7, pp. 229–30

When it comes to taste, Hume is largely a pragmatist. Like subsequent evolutionary psychologists, he believes that we are adapted to take pleasure in what is 'commodious' and 'useful'. Beautiful human beings are healthy, strong, agile, symmetrical, and so fitted for life. Hume's aesthetic is not attuned to the beauty of wilderness and mountains, so much as that of fertile fields and elegant palaces, idealized parks and classical landscapes, nature with her blemishes removed: 'The eye is pleased with the prospect of corn-fields and loaded vineyards; horses grazing, and flocks pasturing: But flies the view of briars and brambles, affording shelter to wolves and serpents' (*EM* 2.9, p. 80). Hume here belongs to the early eighteenth century, before the coming of a taste for the grotesque or the 'sublime'. For the most part, then, the exhibition of 'convenience and utility' rules our verdicts on whether people and things are beautiful. Hume's tastes were conventionally classical or 'Augustan': his supreme model was Homer, and he is more comfortable with ancient writers such as Virgil or Cicero than with freer spirits. He seldom refers to Shakespeare, and one can be fairly sure that he would have been horrified by the Romantics. His criteria are elegance, intelligence, wit, direct expression, classical reference, and a mean between 'refinement' and 'simplicity'.

To see why aesthetics, or what he calls 'taste', is important to Hume we need some context. 'Taste' was a major preoccupation of the eighteenth century. It was a virtue, allied to moral excellence, and an essential qualification for a place in polite society. The qualities of works of art that had to be admired were classical ones: order, harmony, proportion, and 'decency'. Both the emphasis on taste and the kind of taste that was admired can be seen as a defence against a number of anxieties. First, in an age of increasing wealth and consumption, taste was the quality of mind capable of blunting the charge of 'luxury' and idleness. Expenditure was sanctified and redeemed by taste. Taste also provided a lubrication for social mobility: the way the newly rich merchant could eventually climb the hierarchy of society was by conforming to the dictates of taste in his furniture, dress, paintings, or gardens. It had another role in the rejection of Puritan 'enthusiasm', the disordered, tasteless fanaticism of the preceding century. In writers such as the third Earl of Shaftesbury it links itself to virtue, which is no more than taste in behaviour, expressing itself in the social world.

But along with this elevation of taste went a lurking anxiety about taste itself. The journal *The Connoisseur* wrote in 1756 (a year before Hume wrote 'Of the Standard of Taste') that:

> Taste is at present the darling idol of the polite world. The fine
> ladies and gentlemen dress with Taste; the architects, whether
> Gothic or Chinese, build with Taste; the painters paint with Taste;
> critics read with Taste; and in short, fiddlers, players, singers,
> dancers, and mechanics themselves, are all the sons and daugh-
> ters of Taste. Yet in this amazing super-abundancy of Taste, few
> can say what it really is, or what the word itself signifies.[36]

Then as now, there was plenty of rebellion against the tyranny of
taste, and robust satire against its excesses, perhaps anticipating
Pierre Bourdieu's later saying that taste is a 'symbolic violence
perpetrated on the weak by the strong'.[37] The connoisseur is after
all an ambiguous figure, as often a subject of amused contempt as
of admiration. Jean-Jacques Rousseau would shortly lead the
reaction against refinement and civilized taste, in the name of
authenticity and nature: what is normally called taste is what
pleases those who lead us, 'the artists, the wealthy and the great,
and they themselves follow the lead of self interest and pride'.[38]
Hume well understands such scepticism, but his task is to moderate it, without falling into the opposite trap of sounding elitist
or complacent.

The times, then, were ripe for a philosophy of taste, and Hume
returns to it several times in a number of essays, from his very first
of 1742, 'Of the Delicacy of Taste and Passion', through 'Of
Simplicity and Refinement in Writing', to 'Of Tragedy', and
especially in the most influential of them, 'Of the Standard of
Taste'. In spite of the sceptical paragraphs with which this essay
begins, Hume holds that there are virtues of taste. Talking of the
cliché *de gustibus non est disputandum* – there is no disputing about
taste – he says:

> But though this axiom, by passing into a proverb, seems to have
> attained the sanction of common sense; there is certainly a
> species of common sense which opposes it, at least serves to
> modify and restrain it. Whoever would assert an equality of genius
> and elegance between Ogilby and Milton, or Bunyan and Addison,

> would be thought to defend no less an extravagance, than if he
> had maintained a mole-hill to be as high as Teneriffe, or a pond
> as extensive as the ocean. ST 8, pp. 230–1

Hume's examples here are unfortunate: Ogilby is almost entirely
forgotten, but Milton is not widely admired at present either, and
readers who have heard of either of them probably prefer Bunyan
to Addison. But this is irrelevant to Hume's general concern,
which is to vindicate the virtues of the 'man of taste' against the
general background of scepticism about beauty as a real subject
matter.

In the aesthetic sphere just as much as in the moral sphere, there
are 'qualities of mind useful or agreeable to ourselves or others'.
Such qualities are found in various degrees in different persons. So
the problem he sets himself is to understand the nature of these
virtues, and the nature of their authority, against the general background of doubt about whether judgements of beauty and value
represent real, independent qualities of things. It might be noted
that this is almost exactly the same problem that later confronted
Kant when he came to write the *Critique of Judgement*, his own
attempt to understand aesthetics.

Our encounters with beautiful things and people give us pleasure, so in the first instance we are talking about things we find
pleasant. Hume says in the *Treatise*:

> If we consider all the hypotheses, which have been formed either
> by philosophy or common reason, to explain the difference
> betwixt beauty and deformity, we shall find that all of them
> resolve into this, that beauty is such an order and construction of
> parts, as either by the *primary constitution* of our nature, by
> *custom*, or by *caprice*, is fitted to give a pleasure and satisfaction
> to the soul. This is the distinguishing character of beauty, and
> forms all the difference betwixt it and deformity, whose natural
> tendency is to produce uneasiness. Pleasure and pain, therefore,
> are not only necessary attendants of beauty and deformity, but
> constitute their very essence. (*T* II.i.8, p. 299)

So the essay starts with two opposing thoughts, each of which has great appeal, yet that seem inconsistent with each other. On the one hand we have the line that issues in the motto that beauty lies in the eye of the beholder, and the related proverb that *de gustibus non est disputandum*. On the other hand we have the practice of criticism, and the various ways in which we suppose that one taste is better than another, or that we can be mistaken or at fault in the ways in which we respond to works of literature or works of art. We deploy criteria of success, and indeed not only the critic, but the artist striving for an outcome, has the idea of possible success or failure, of striving for work that hits the mark, and of discontent with work that misses it. The process of creation, as well as that of estimation and judgement (which goes along with it), requires submission to such a thought. Otherwise there would be nothing for the artist to try to do. Someone might say that this conception is missing from modern art ('My four-year-old could do that'), but that is exactly why so much is so often meaningless and dispiriting.

Hume sets about reconciling the two opposing thoughts by reminding us of the 'test of time'. Some works gain a temporary popularity, only to fade away and be forgotten. Others, like Homer, endure through every other fluctuation of taste and opinion. So there are works that are somehow 'fitted' to arouse sentiments of esteem, admiration, and pleasure. The task of the good critic will be to put himself in a state that enables such works to have their effect.

For this to happen there are certain conditions to be met. First, the critic must be in a sound state:

A man in a fever would not insist on his palate as able to decide concerning flavours; nor would one, affected with the jaundice, pretend to give a verdict with regard to colours. In each creature, there is a sound and a defective state; and the former alone can be supposed to afford us a true standard of a taste and sentiment. (*ST* 12, pp. 233–4)

This sound state includes 'a perfect serenity of mind, a recollection of thought, a due attention to the object', as necessary for disinterested and engaged perception of a work. After that there are four virtues of the critic to notice: sensitivity or delicacy of discrimination; a background of practice, and particularly practice in making comparisons; freedom from prejudice; and finally 'good sense' or strong understanding. And although he does not stress it in his essay, under good sense we can suppose Hume to include the kinds of sensitivity, particularly delicate and practised imagination and sympathy, which are necessary across the board to our understanding of each other.

Each of the qualities on Hume's list of virtues may seem to belong to a rhetoric of refinement, as if he is naively putting himself in the target area for democrats like Rousseau or Bourdieu. Yet he is surely correct that a person who can't tell one work from another, or who is completely new to a kind of work, or who has prejudices that determine him in advance to like or dislike some work, or who is what Hume would have called a blockhead, is not someone whose opinion is likely to deserve much attention. And this has nothing to do with elitism: the rock star or rap poet would only listen to critics or judges of their work who meet these requirements.

So what is the judge or critic trying to do? One straightforward answer, suggested for instance by Hume's talk of the 'catholic and universal beauty', would be that the work does possess some degree of beauty or merit, and it is the critic's job to estimate it. But this is foreign to Hume's theory of value, here and everywhere. It ignores the power of the sceptical attack on any casual introduction of the 'real value' of things, and Hume's own adherence to the species of philosophy that says that 'no sentiment represents what is really in the object'. Hume never repudiates the sentimentalist doctrines of the first six paragraphs of the essay. His effort is to defend the practice of criticism in the face of them.

Some of Hume's phrasing suggests a different but equally simple answer: the critic is trying to anticipate or second-guess the verdict of the ages. That is, he is to treat himself as a likely indicator of the judgements of other people across time. Taste would be, as Rousseau phrased it, the faculty of judging what pleases or displeases the greatest number. It would be as if I approached a general election, saying that *I* like candidate X, so I expect other people do so as well, and I therefore predict that he will get elected. I believe myself to be typical enough that my reactions are the ones I can expect to be widely shared. Although this view has been attributed to Hume, it is clearly not his. As you react to a painting or a work of literature, you are not taking a flyer on whether most people think like you. If I offer the verdict, 'Big Brother is disgusting,' I am not guessing that the majority of viewers think it is disgusting – in fact, I may know they love it. As Kant later put it in the *Critique of Judgement*, talking of what he called the judgement of beauty, the appraisal is not that people *do* like or dislike the work, but that they *should*: 'The assertion is not that everyone *will* fall in with our judgement, but that everyone *ought* to agree with it.'[39]

The view is also deeply unsatisfactory, since as an account of what the critic or judge is trying to do it only works by passing the buck. That is, the theory holds that the critic is trying to anticipate the verdict of other critics or the public. And what is the nature of *those* verdicts? Are they trying to anticipate the verdict of other critics – who in turn are doing the same?

Finally, the account fits badly with the prominence Hume accords to the special virtues of the good critic. This is the whole point of a demographic view, in Rousseau's eyes: it is reinstating the rights of the majority, the vulgar, against the tyranny of the educated, the civilized, or the elite. But that is not an axe that Hume is grinding. Consider delicacy of taste, for example. Hume illustrates this with the story from *Don Quixote* of the kinsmen of Sancho Panza who established their credentials as wine tasters by detecting the most minute taint in a hogshead of wine. The one complained of a taint of leather, and the other of a taint of iron, and when the hogshead (all fifty-four gallons) was emptied, sure enough at the bottom there was an iron key with a leather thong. This is a remarkable delicacy, sure enough, but just because of that it would actually disqualify these virtuosi from a purely demographic role, that is, from being predictors of the verdicts or reactions of other people. If they took their own reactions as indicative, they would predict that others would dislike the wine, but they would be wrong because most people wouldn't taste either the iron or the leather. Similarly, the person who is unusually practised, or who has a wider range of comparison than most, or who is blessed with greater good sense, is thereby untypical, and actually *disqualified* from regarding himself as a kind of one-man focus group.[40]

So the question remains: what is the critic up to? Where does the 'ought' come from, and why should we listen to it? For Hume this transposes to the question of why the virtues of the critic are genuinely virtues, and as we have seen, the answer has to be in terms of their value to us, perhaps only imprecisely indicated by their 'agreeableness' and 'utility'.

One helpful account is offered in the early essay, 'Of the Delicacy of Taste and Passion'. Here Hume talks of a quivering sensitivity to the pleasures and pains of life, that makes up the person of delicate passions. On the whole, such a sensibility is a curse. Too much goes wrong in life, and it is better to treat the whole thing as more of a joke, to lighten up. But delicacy of taste is another matter. The pleasures and pains of life are largely beyond our control, so if we react extravagantly to them, we will often be upset, gloomy, melancholy. But delicacy of taste is exercised on things over which we do have control, such as which books to read:

> There is a *delicacy* of *taste* observable in some men, which very much resembles this *delicacy* of *passion*, and produces the same sensibility to beauty and deformity of every kind, as that does to prosperity and adversity, obligations and injuries ... A polite and judicious conversation affords him the highest entertainment; rudeness or impertinence is as great a punishment to him. In short, delicacy of taste has the same effect as delicacy of passion: It enlarges the sphere both of our happiness and misery, and makes us sensible to pains as well as pleasures, which escape the rest of mankind ...
>
> When a man is possessed of that talent, he is more happy by

what pleases his taste, than by what gratifies his appetites, and
receives more enjoyment from a poem or a piece of reasoning
than the most expensive luxury can afford. ('Of the Delicacy of
Taste and Passion', *EMP*, pp. 4–5)

So the person of delicate taste has sources of pleasure unknown to
the coarser majority. Furthermore, delicacy of taste largely inocu-
lates us against disturbing strength of feeling, giving us a 'juster'
view of what actually deserves to excite us and what does not. In
fact, Hume says, we can go further. It is not just that the delights
of literature and the other arts subdue life's passions, but rather
they strengthen the best and suppress the worst: 'They draw off the
mind from the hurry of business and interest; cherish reflection;
dispose to tranquillity; and produce an agreeable melancholy,
which, of all dispositions of the mind, is the best suited to love and
friendship.' So the traits of mind that characterize the good critic
are indeed useful or agreeable to himself.

We might not be entirely convinced about this, but then we
might also find it difficult to do better than Hume in saying what
is so good about art and literature. The connoisseur may get more
enjoyment out of his practice, perhaps, but as Hume also notices,
delicacy of taste may itself be a source of discontent, as fewer and
fewer things are allowed to measure up. Indeed, Hume is generally
more democratic about enjoyment:

Objects have absolutely no worth or value in themselves. They
derive their worth merely from the passion [we bring to them]. If
that be strong, and steady, and successful, the person is happy.
It cannot reasonably be doubted, but a little miss, dressed in a
new gown for a dancing-school ball, receives as compleat enjoyment as the greatest orator, who triumphs in the spendor of his
eloquence, while he governs the passions and resolutions of a
numerous assembly. ('The Sceptic', *EMP*, p. 166)

So we cannot really rely on the extra dose of enjoyment that good
judgement will bring to its possessor, since the connoisseur ravished

by, say, a piece of exquisite porcelain, like the triumphant orator, may be matched or overtaken, in point of pleasure, by the little miss in her new gown or admiring her new doll.

Hume would do better to say that exercising a practised, delicate judgement is also the exercise of an *ability*, and thus a source of *pride* in oneself, and general *esteem* and *admiration* from others. Furthermore, in many cases these abilities are aspects of abilities that have a wider application. An ear or eye for the sentimental and the false, the pompous and the vainglorious in art is at least the close sibling of a similar eye or ear for those qualities in everyday life. This is part of the standard defence of literature as an education and a focal point for emotional growth. Bitter twentieth-century experience notwithstanding, it is an accomplishment to be able to locate the features whereby one poem achieves sincerity whereas another rings false, and an accomplishment that has the power to spill over, sensitizing us to the declamatory falsities of demagogues and charlatans. It is not compulsory to work at such accomplishments, and they may not even be detected as such by those who have not got them. But they are merits for all that, and a proper source of quiet pride in those who have them. One wouldn't care to be without them, having once attained some proficiency, any more than one would care to lose what one knows about history or mathematics, or the ability to write a grammatical sentence. Once we have obtained some abilities in such a direction, we will look back on our previous state, when we were cloth-eared or blind, deaf to the language or simply confused, with some embarrassment.

Hume's insistence that practice is necessary to educate taste, and that comparisons are needed before we can judge a kind of work, gets a charming application in the *Dialogues*. Philo is arguing that if you use the argument to design you renounce any right to believe that the deity (or deities) you arrive at is (or are) perfect. For you have absolutely no reason to suppose the world is perfect:

> Could a peasant, if the *Aeneid* were read to him, pronounce that
> poem to be absolutely faultless, or even assign to it its proper

rank among the productions of human wit; he, who had never
seen any other production? (*D* 5.6)

The point here being that having only the one world to go on, we
are in absolutely no position to say whether it is especially good or
bad of its kind.

Hume returns to the question of diversity of taste towards the
end of the essay, when he argues that we should expect such diversity to arise from harmless causes: 'diversity in the internal frame
or external situation as is entirely blameless on both sides' (*ST* 28,
p. 244). These differences may arise from various causes, including
the different tastes we have at different ages of life, or in virtue of
difference of circumstances. Such diversity should not provoke dis-
putes about the relative merits of works, however:

> It is plainly an error in a critic, to confine his approbation to one
> species or style of writing, and condemn all the rest. But it is
> almost impossible not to feel a predilection for that which suits
> our particular turn and disposition. Such preferences are innocent
> and unavoidable, and can never reasonably be the object of dis-
> pute, because there is no standard, by which they can be
> decided. (*ST* 30, p. 244)

Similarly, we may have a predilection for the manners and dress of
our own times, but 'Must we throw aside the pictures of our
ancestors, because of their ruffs and fardingales?' (*ST* 32, p. 246).[41]
The implication is that this would be mere partiality or prejudice
in our own favour, and rightly or wrongly, Hume is certain that
there is all the difference between a prepared mind and a preju-
diced one.

Among preferences which are not innocent are those due to
perverted morality:

> But where the ideas of morality and decency alter from one age to
> another, and where vicious manners are described, without being
> marked with the proper characters of blame and disapprobation;

this must be allowed to disfigure the poem, and to be a real
deformity. I cannot, nor is it proper I should, enter into such sentiments. *ST* 32, pp. 246

We can easily appreciate the point if we think of the distaste we
feel for works that casually endorse racist or sexist attitudes,
common at previous times but regretted and disowned at the present.

Hume's essay is, in my view, a brilliant success, defending the
practices of connoisseurship and criticism against the sceptic's
charge that they have no subject matter. Exactly as with ethics, we
begin with a natural endowment inclining us towards some things
and against others, and then we find that with practice we 'get our
eye in', and the exercise of judgement becomes a pleasure in itself,
and a valued component of the good life. The practice stands on
its own feet: it is not to be thought of as a means to getting at 'the
truth' about an object's beauty, and we risk misleading ourselves if
we speak in those terms, but it has its own value and delivers its
own pleasures.

Hume very much hoped that people of taste would enjoy his
writings. He liked to portray himself as an 'ambassador from the
dominions of learning to those of conversation' ('Of Essay
Writing', *EMP*, p. 535). But of course he is more than that. On all
the topics we have considered, he is either the most profound
thinker of the modern world, or if not, then at least occupies the
very front rank. His understanding of human nature was clear-
eyed and unflinching, yet also infused with an imperturbable
benevolence. His humanity is exemplary, and his voice is one that
needs to be heard in speculation and controversy well beyond the
confines of academic philosophy. It is safe to say that the world of
conversation is always in need of such an embassy, and such an
ambassador.

NOTES

1 Immanuel Kant, *Prologomena to Any Future Metaphysics* (1783), ed. Henry Allison and Peter Heath, in Immanuel Kant, *Theoretical Philosophy after 1781* (Cambridge: Cambridge University Press, 2002), p. 56.
2 If it is, help is to hand at Jonathan Bennett's website: www.earlymod-erntexts.com, where updated English translations are to be found.
3 On the celebration of reason as the point of resemblance between man and God in the century before Hume, see Edward Craig, *The Mind of God and the Works of Man* (Oxford: Oxford University Press, 1987), ch. 1.
4 Immanuel Kant, *The Critique of Pure Reason* (A 1781, B 1787), trans. Norman Kemp Smith (London: Macmillan, 1963), A371–2. See also A378.
5 See, for example, Richard Rorty, *Consequences of Pragmatism* (Brighton: Harvester, 1982).
6 Thomas Reid, *Inquiry into the Human Mind, on the Principles of Common Sense*, in *The Works of Thomas Reid*, ed. William Hamilton, 8th ed. (Edinburgh: James Thin, 1895), vol. 1, p. 102.
7 Friedrich Nietzsche, *The Genealogy of Morals* (1887), in *The Birth of Tragedy and The Genealogy of Morals*, trans. Francis Golffing (New York: Doubleday, 1956), Third Essay, §12.
8 The key works are Ludwig Wittgenstein, *Philosophical Investigations* (Oxford: Blackwell, 1953), and Wilfrid Sellars, *Empiricism and the Philosophy of Mind* (Cambridge, Mass.: Harvard University Press, 1956, reissued 1997).
9 I put the term 'Cartesian' in inverted commas, because the extent to which Descartes himself was, in this sense, a Cartesian is disputable.
10 This is well argued in Steven Everson, 'The Difference between Feeling and Thinking', *Mind*, 97 (July 1988), pp. 401–13.
11 William James, *Principles of Psychology* (1890) (Cambridge, Mass.: Harvard University Press, 1981), p. 462; Kant, *Critique of Pure Reason*, A156, B195.
12 Wittgenstein's so-called rule-following considerations occupy *Philosophical Investigations*, from approximately §140 to §204.

13 Kant, *Critique of Pure Reason*, A51, B75.

14 George Berkeley, *A Treatise Concerning the Principles of Human Knowledge* (1710), ed. Jonathan Dancy (Oxford: Oxford University Press, 1998), §§25–6.

15 The distinguished Hume scholar Norman Kemp Smith gives abundant evidence that Hume was in fact led to his theory of causation by reflection on this parallel view of morality. See *The Philosophy of David Hume* (London: Macmillan, 1941), pp. 14–51. See also ch. 6 below.

16 The fountainhead of much work on the psychology of causal perception is A. Michotte, *The Perception of Causality* (New York: Basic Books, 1963). Some of the flavour is entertainingly seen at cogweb.ucla.edu/Discourse/Narrative/michotte-demo.swf.

17 Jonathan Bennett, *Locke, Berkeley, Hume: Central Themes* (Oxford: Oxford University Press, 1971), p. 313.

18 John Locke, *An Essay Concerning Human Understanding* (1690), ed. P. H. Nidditch (Oxford: Oxford University Press, 1975), bk II, ch. ix, pp. 143–9.

19 George Berkeley, *Three Dialogues between Hylas and Philonous* (1713), ed. Jonathan Dancy (Oxford: Oxford University Press, 1998), Dialogue II, p. 97.

20 A good modern anthology of writings promoting, attacking, or qualifying this kind of view is Tamar Szabó Gendler and John Hawthorne, eds., *Perceptual Experience* (Oxford: Oxford University Press, 2006).

21 Locke, *Essay*, bk II, ch. xxvii, pp. 335–41.

22 *The Letters of David Hume*, ed. J. Y. T. Greig (Oxford: Oxford University Press, 1932), vol. 1, letter 73, p. 158. The question of how different the doctrines of the two texts are still excites commentators.

23 For a primer, see my *Think* (Oxford: Oxford University Press, 1999), ch. 4.

24 Kant, *Critique of Pure Reason*, B131–2.

25 Friedrich Nietzsche, *Writings from the Late Notebooks*, ed. Rüdiger Bittner, trans. Kate Sturge (Cambridge: Cambridge University Press, 2003), pp. 20–1.

26 For readers unfamiliar with the prisoners' dilemma, there are many good introductions, including Brian Skyrms, *The Stag Hunt and the Evolution of Social Structure* (Cambridge: Cambridge University Press, 2004).

27 For example, David Lewis allows that the theory of games, which provides the technical heart of his book on convention, is but 'scaffolding', and the theory that emerges is in effect that of Hume. David Lewis, *Convention* (Cambridge, Mass.: Harvard University Press, 1969), p. 3.

28 See, for example, Thomas Hobbes, *Leviathan* (1651), ed. J. C. A. Gaskin (Oxford: Oxford University Press, 1998); John Locke, *Two*

Treatises of Government (1689), ed. P. Laslett (Cambridge: Cambridge University Press, 1988); Jean-Jacques Rousseau, *The Social Contract* (1762), in *Discourse on Political Economy and The Social Contract*, trans. C. Betts (Oxford: Oxford University Press, 1999).

29 David Hume, 'My Own Life', *EMP*, p. xxxvi

30 Letter to the Reverend George Campbell, 7 June 1762, in *Letters*, vol. 1, letter 194, pp. 360–1.

31 Robert Fogelin's excellent *A Defense of Hume on Miracles* (Princeton: Princeton University Press, 2003) magisterially demolishes some of the more ludicrous or abject recent misreadings. It is of course an irony not lost on Hume's admirers that where the seas of emotion start to rise, in connection with religion, morals, or politics, the cognitive functions of dissenters lose their bearings entirely.

32 Edward Gibbon, *The Decline and Fall of the Roman Empire* (1776) (London: Dent, 1993), vol. 1, ch. 15, p. 566.

33 If we were not, would we ever get to rely on testimony at all, since it is not feasible for us to perform actual checks in every case, or even many cases? See A. Coady, *Testimony* (Oxford: Oxford University Press, 1992), and also Jennifer Lackey and Ernest Sosa, eds., *The Epistemology of Testimony* (Oxford: Oxford University Press, 2006).

34 Donald Gillies, 'Was Bayes a Bayesian?', *Historia Mathematica*, 14 (1987), pp. 325–46. See also Philip Dawid and Donald Gillies, 'A Bayesian Analysis of Hume's Argument Concerning Miracles', *The Philosophical Quarterly*, 39 (1989), pp. 57–69. I take readers through an elementary introduction to Bayes's theorem in *Think*, pp. 218–25.

35 'Letter from Adam Smith, LL.D. to William Strahan, Esq.', *EMP*, p. xlvi.

36 George Colman, *The Connoisseur*, no. 120, 13 May 1756. Collected in *The Connoisseur: By Mr Town, Critic and Censor-General* (London: R. Baldwin, 1756), vol. 2, p. 721.

37 Pierre Bourdieu, *Distinction: A Social Critique of Judgment and Taste* (London: Routledge, 1984), p. 165.

38 Jean-Jacques Rousseau, *Émile, or Education* (1762), trans. Barbara Foxley (London: Dent, 1974), p. 306.

39 Immanuel Kant, *The Critique of the Power of Judgement* (1790), trans. Paul Guyer and Eric Matthews (Cambridge: Cambridge University Press, 2000), p. 123. Kant distinguishes sharply between the 'judgement of beauty' which has this 'normative' force, and mere judgements that things are agreeable, which according to him has none. Hume, sensibly, has no such dualism, any more than he does in the parallel moral context.

40 In P. G. Wodehouse's story, 'The Episode of the Dog McIntosh' (originally published in *Very Good, Jeeves* in 1930), the philistine theatre

producer uses his ghastly nine-year-old child as a good indicator of the taste of the public. On the demographic view, we would have to say that the child exhibits excellent taste.

41 A 'fardingale' or farthingale is a hooped petticoat used to extend the volume of women's skirts.

CHRONOLOGY

1711 Hume born on 26 April, and raised at Ninewells, the family estate in Berwickshire.

1722–5 Attends Edinburgh University (perhaps until 1726).

1726–9 Studies law and literature.

1729–34 Engages in private philosophical study, and plans design of the *Treatise*.

1734 Spends a brief period in Bristol as a bank clerk, then moves to Paris.

1734–5 Resident in Rheims.

1735–7 Writes the *Treatise* in the academy town of La Flèche in Anjou, France.

1737–9 Returns to London to prepare the *Treatise* for publication.

1739 Books I and II of the *Treatise* published. Hume returns to Scotland.

1740 Book III of the *Treatise* published. *Abstract* published as a defence.

1741 First volume of *Essays Moral and Political* published.

1742 Second volume of *Essays* published.

1745 Fails to obtain the chair of Ethics and Pneumatical Philosophy at Edinburgh. Becomes private tutor to the (mad) Marquess of Annandale. Second Scottish Jacobite Rebellion under Bonnie Prince Charlie.

1746 Becomes secretary to Lieutenant-General James St Clair; accompanies him on an expedition to Brittany.

1747 Returns to Ninewells; prepares a third edition of *Essays Moral and Political*.

1748 *Philosophical Essays Concerning Human Understanding* (from 1758 known as the *Enquiry Concerning Human Understanding*) published in London: three editions issued in the subsequent three years.

1748 Accompanies St Clair as aide-de-camp on secret diplomatic missions to Vienna and Turin.

1751 *Enquiry Concerning the Principles of Morals* published. Hume moves from Ninewells to Edinburgh.

1752 *Political Discourses* published. Hume fails to obtain the Chair of Logic at Glasgow. Elected Keeper of the Advocates' Library in Edinburgh.

1754 First volume of the *History of England* published. Five subsequent volumes appear at intervals until 1762.

1755–6 The Church of Scotland mounts an unsuccessful campaign to have Hume excommunicated.

1757 *Four Dissertations*, including the *Natural History of Religion*, published.

1763–5 Hume is appointed secretary to the British ambassador to Paris, Lord Hertford, and is lionized in the salons of Paris. Grows opulent and corpulent.

1766 Invites Jean-Jacques Rousseau, forced to flee France, to England, but Rousseau's paranoia leads to a rupture in their relations.

1772 Hume's health begins to fail.

1776 Death of Hume on 25 August.

1779 Posthumous publication of the *Dialogues Concerning Natural Religion*.

BIBLIOGRAPHY

Hume's works cited

A Treatise of Human Nature, ed. L. A. Selby-Bigge, 2nd ed. revised by P. H. Nidditch. Oxford: Oxford University Press, 1978.

Abstract of A Treatise of Human Nature, in *A Treatise of Human Nature*, ed. David Fate Norton and Mary Jay Norton. Oxford: Oxford University Press, 2000, pp. 4–17.

An Enquiry Concerning Human Understanding, ed. Tom L. Beauchamp. Oxford: Oxford University Press, 1999.

An Enquiry Concerning the Principles of Morals, ed. Tom L. Beauchamp. Oxford: Oxford University Press, 1998.

Essays: Moral, Political, and Literary, ed. Eugene F. Miller. Indianapolis: Liberty Fund, 1985.

Dialogues Concerning Natural Religion, ed. Dorothy Coleman. Cambridge: Cambridge University Press, 2007.

The Letters of David Hume, ed. J. Y. T. Greig, 2 vols. Oxford: Oxford University Press, 1932.

Secondary literature

This bibliography includes only some of the best-known books on Hume's philosophy. Other resources include back numbers of the journal *Hume Studies*, and a vast number of other papers and collections of papers.

Baier, Annette C. *A Progress of Sentiments: Reflections on Hume's Treatise*. Cambridge, Mass.: Harvard University Press, 1991.

Beebee, Helen. *Hume on Causation*. Abingdon: Routledge, 2006.

Bennett, Jonathan. *Locke, Berkeley, Hume: Central Themes*. Oxford: Oxford University Press, 1971.

Burns, R. M. *The Great Debate on Miracles*. Lewisburg: Bucknell University Press, 1981.

Dicker, Georges. *Hume's Epistemology and Metaphysics*. London: Routledge, 1998.

Fogelin, Robert, *A Defence of Hume on Miracles*. Princeton: Princeton University Press, 2003.

—— *Hume's Skepticism in the Treatise of Human Nature*. London: Routledge, 1985.

Garrett, Don. *Cognition and Commitment in Hume's Philosophy*. Oxford: Oxford University Press, 1997.

Gaskin, J. C. A. *Hume's Philosophy of Religion*, 2nd ed. Basingstoke: Macmillan, 1988.

Holden, T. *The Architecture of Matter: Galileo to Kant*. Oxford: Oxford University Press, 2004.

Houston, J. *Reported Miracles: A Critique of Hume*. Cambridge: Cambridge University Press, 1994.

Jones, Peter. *Hume's Sentiments*. Edinburgh: Edinburgh University Press, 1982.

Kemp Smith, Norman. *The Philosophy of David Hume*. London: Macmillan, 1941).

Millican, Peter. *Reading Hume on Human Understanding*. Oxford: Oxford University Press, 2002.

Noonan, Harold W. *Hume on Knowledge*. London: Routledge, 1999.

Norton, David Fate, ed. *The Cambridge Companion to Hume*. Cambridge: Cambridge University Press, 1993.

Noxon, James. *Hume's Philosophical Development*. Oxford: Oxford University Press, 1973.

Owen, David. *Hume's Reason*. Oxford: Oxford University Press, 1999.

Passmore, John. *Hume's Intentions*, 3rd ed. London: Duckworth, 1980, ch. 2.

Pears, David., *Hume's System*. Oxford: Oxford University Press, 1990.

Price, H. H. *Hume's Theory of the External World*. Oxford: Oxford University Press, 1940.

Russell, Paul. *Freedom and Moral Sentiment*. Oxford: Oxford University Press, 1995.

INDEX